走吧!
一起用英语
去旅行!

林雨薇 | 著

北京理工大学出版社
BEIJING INSTITUTE OF TECHNOLOGY PRESS

使用这本书的方式

适用对象
1. 具备初级英语听说、阅读能力的人
2. 计划去国外旅游的人

使用时机
1. 出国前针对基本语言能力及旅游情况进行准备
2. 带出国，在酒店临时恶补，或是放进包带出门随时查阅

★ 旅行一定会说到的会话！

体验人文风土民情！
出国一定要去的景点，绝对不能错过。

游客服务中心

游客服务中心在哪里？	Where is the visitors center?
在车站的二楼。	It's on the second floor of the station.
顺着标识走就可以找到了。	Just follow the sign and you can ... it.
请问有免费地图可以领取吗？	Excuse me, are there any free maps to get?
我可以拿一份观光导览手册吗？	Can I take a travel guide?
请问有中文版的旅游手册吗？	Excuse me, is there a Chinese travel guide?
旅游手册在那里，请自行取用。	Travel guides are over there. Ple... be free to get.
我想询问旅游一日券的事情。	I'd like to ask about the one day ... voucher.
我需要走路还是坐地铁呢？	Do I need to walk or take the subway?

对话框说明

蓝绿色底框 + 绿色字
↳ 表示非常重要的会话！

浅绿色底框 / 白色底框 → 表示一组对话

黄色 / 浅黄色 → 表示一定要会的会话

- 一定要会的基本会话
- 会话内容涵盖各种情境
- 以中文句为主，方便读者查找
- 美籍老师精心录制 MP3（录制内容为会话及单词）
  ★ 本书附赠音频为MP3格式。

User's Guide

★ 套上单词即可使用的万用句型

- 简短、实用的万能句型
- 可套用到句型里的单词
- 句型及替换的单词皆补充
- 替换的单词补充实景照片

★ 在国外自助旅行一定会看到听到用到的单词

- 在国外生活、游玩一定会用到的单词
- 单词皆补充美式国际音标
- 单词搭配实景照片,更容易对照记忆
- 单词录音方式为 左→右 上→下

★ 旅游资讯与文化

- 补充最实用的旅游资讯,提供行程规划的参考
- 讲述旅游中要知道的外国文化

加拿大

加拿大位于北美洲的北部，和美国相连。加拿大是由十个省、三个地区组成的联邦，首都为渥太华，最大的城市是多伦多，官方语言为英语和法语，货币为加拿大元（C$ / CAD）。

英国

英国由英格兰、苏格兰、威尔士、北爱尔兰四个地区组成。其政权为君主立宪制，其政治体制为议会制，首都是伦敦，"威斯敏斯特唐宁街10号"是首相官邸，官方语言为英语，货币为英镑（£/GBP）。

澳大利亚

澳大利亚位于南半球，是全球面积第六大的国家，也是全球唯一独占一个大陆的国家，首都为堪培拉，最大的城市是悉尼，官方语言为英语，货币为澳元（$/AUD）。

新西兰

新西兰由两大岛屿（北岛、南岛）组成，两个岛以库克海峡作为分隔，首都为惠灵顿（位于北岛），最大的城市是奥克兰，官方语言为英语，货币为新西兰元（NZ$/NZD）。

Chapter 1 出发前 ▶001
- 赴美旅游资讯介绍 ▶002
- 一定要会的招呼语 ▶009

Chapter 2 机场相关 ▶015
- 走吧!出发去旅行! ▶016
  [情境] 订机票、柜台报到、行李托运、安全检查、免税店、候机室
- 顺利抵达目的地了! ▶026
  [情境] 准备登机、飞机服务、飞机餐点、入境、领取行李、离开机场

Chapter 3 国外住宿 ▶037
- 先去酒店办理入住吧! ▶038
  [情境] 订房、登记入住、房间介绍、早餐介绍、询问服务、酒店与周围环境
- 退房!往下个地点前进! ▶050
  [情境] 客房服务、寻求帮忙、赞美及抱怨、办理退房、遗忘物品、特殊要求

Chapter 4 观光景点 ▶059
- 体验人文风土民情! ▶060
  [情境] 游客服务中心、博物馆、展览馆、艺廊、教堂
- 徜徉在自然美景中! ▶072
  [情境] 风景名胜、赏枫、赏雪、冲浪、泛舟、一日旅行团、乘船观光、搭直升机、纪念品专卖店

Chapter 5 异国美食 ▶087
- 去餐厅吃美食吧! ▶088
  [情境] 传统美食、海鲜自助餐、特殊需求、下午茶、咖啡店
- 超级市场也有好吃的! ▶102
  [情境] 超级市场、鲜食类、饼干糖果类、面包甜点类、饮料类、购买须知

- 去小酒馆干一杯！▶116
  [情境] 小酒馆、比萨店、酒水类、早餐店、牛排馆、座位、结账、表达不满、表达赞扬

Chapter 6 购物乐趣 ▶131

- 去百货公司大采购！▶132
  [情境] 百货公司服务台、百货公司专柜/品牌专卖店、试穿、结账、退税、产品内容、退换货
- 药妆店是女孩们的最爱！▶146
  [情境] 药妆店美妆区、药妆店保养区、药妆店咨询区、药妆店药品区、药妆店柜台、药店服务、美甲店、美体美容店

Chapter 7 国外交通 ▶165

- 四通八达的地铁系统！▶166
  [情境] 买票、自动售票机、询问时刻、询问路线、询问月台、询问车站环境
- 饱览街道风光的巴士！▶180
  [情境] 公交车、出租车、人力车、游览船、马车、自行车、租车

Chapter 8 紧急状况 ▶191

- 寄信、取钱，一次搞定！▶192
  [情境] 银行提款、换钱、汇钱、寄件、信用卡挂失、信用卡刷卡、支票兑现、彩票
- 不怕一万，只怕万一！▶200
  [情境] 东西丢失、遭到盗窃、证件遗失、发生意外、生病就医、打电话

Chapter 1 出发前

本书以美国作为主要的旅游目的地,出发前,先了解一下美国这个国家吧!除了对美国的国情、节庆、大都市进行基本介绍之外,在章节最后补充了适用全世界的不可不知的旅游会话。

I want to go to...

赴美旅游资讯介绍

介绍美国

美利坚合众国（the United States of America），简称美国，英文的简称有：the United States、America、the States，缩写可写成：the U.S.A. 或 the U.S.。

基本资讯

人 口 数	3.257 亿
官方语言	英语
国家结构	联邦制
国家政权	三权分立：行政——总统 　　　　　立法——国会 　　　　　司法——最高法院
主要宗教	基督教
首　　都	华盛顿哥伦比亚特区
地理最高点	麦金利山
最长河流	密西西比河
时　　区	美国时区，西 5 至西 10 区
电　　压	110V
道路通行方向	靠右行驶

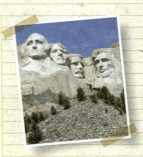

美国货币

纸　币

美国目前流通的纸币面额有 100 美元、50 美元、20 美元、10 美元、5 美元、2 美元、1 美元。历史上曾经发行过 500 美元、1000 美元、5000 美元、10000 美元、100000 美元面额的钞票，但现在已不再使用。

硬　币

美国的硬币分为 1 美元、50 美分、25 美分、10 美分、5 美分、1 美分。

出发前

机场相关

国外住宿

观光景点

异国美食

购物乐趣

国外交通

紧急状况

美国食物

美国是多民族国家,以人口占比来看,白人约占总人口的64%,其余分别为拉美裔、非洲裔、亚裔等,亚裔又包括菲律宾裔美国人、中国裔美国人、印度裔美国人、越南裔美国人、日本裔美国人、韩国裔美国人等。

在这样的文化背景下,美国的食物种类非常丰富,各地区也因为文化背景等因素而具有地方化的特色,例如美国南方的饮食就和北方饮食不大一样。

汉堡(hamburger / burger)

圆形面包内夹有馅料,馅料以汉堡排(一般为牛肉)为主,配料则以生菜、番茄、洋葱、腌制小菜、奶酪为主,通常也会淋上番茄酱、芥末酱、蛋黄酱等调味酱。

热狗(hot dog)

基本上为夹有香肠的面包,香肠一般为牛肉或猪肉的,有些店家可能会先以烟熏的方式制作热狗。热狗的制作方式是将生菜、碎洋葱、切片或切丁的番茄放入面包中作为基底,再放上香肠,最后在热狗上淋上番茄酱、芥末酱等调味酱,也可搭配奶酪或是辣肉酱食用。

水牛城辣鸡翅(buffalo wings / wings)

利用鸡翅的中下部位,不裹面粉,直接油炸,再加上以辣椒为主的酱汁进行调味。在餐厅点餐时,可依据喜好的口味点选辣度(suicidal、hot、medium、mild)。各家主厨针对口味进行创新研发,因此每家餐厅供应的辣鸡翅都各有特色。

炸热狗(corn dog)

将热狗裹上玉米粉后油炸,通常会插上竹签以方便食用。

苹果派(apple pie)

若提到美国代表性的甜食,就非苹果派莫属了。苹果派的历史悠久,在一些惯用语、广告语中都会看到苹果派的身影。苹果派主要是以切碎的苹果为配料,佐以糖、肉桂、肉豆蔻或葡萄干等调味,并在表面覆盖馅饼皮后烤制而成。

美国体育运动

美国人很重视体育活动,大多数人会参与或观看体育比赛。在美国最受欢迎的三大体育运动分别是:棒球、篮球以及橄榄球。也因为美国人对于运动的重视,相关的体育组织也蓬勃发展。

棒球(baseball)

棒球在美国是非常普及的运动,美国最高级的职业棒球联赛为:美国职业棒球大联盟(Major League Baseball,缩写为MLB),简称美国职棒或大联盟。目前共有30支球队参与,其赛季从每年的四月持续到十月。除大联盟之外,还有"美国职业棒球小联盟(MiLB)"。

篮球(basketball)

美国职业篮球联赛(National Basketball Association,缩写为NBA)总共有30支球队,分成东部联盟与西部联盟,每个联盟由三个赛区组成,每个赛区有5支球队。赛季从每年十月月底开始,分为常规赛和季后赛两部分。球队在常规赛中争取进入季后赛的资格,而季后赛的最后一轮也称为"总决赛",将由两个联盟的冠军争夺NBA的总冠军头衔。

橄榄球(national football)

美国人对于橄榄球的喜爱度远超过棒球。在美国各高中、大学也都有橄榄球队。主要举办职业美式足球赛的美国国家橄榄球联盟(National Football League,缩写NFL)总共有32支球队,其冠军赛"超级杯"转播时,超过一半的美国家庭会在电视前收看,而全世界有超过150个国家转播比赛,可以说是全美收视率最高的体育赛事。

美国签证

美国的签证主要可分成两大类:

❶ 移民签证:永久居留于美国(即绿卡)。

❷ 非移民签证:入境美国并短暂停留,停留期满后即离开美国。

由于申请美国签证的步骤较为烦琐,所需的时间也较长,不同的身份以及入境目的各有对应的签证类型,建议可先上美国驻华大使馆的网站查阅相关信息,也可以打电话咨询。

美国知名城市介绍

[纽约] New York

纽约是美国人口最多的城市，在商业与金融上具有巨大的全球影响力，华尔街的一点风声会影响全球的经济脉动。因为联合国总部设立在纽约市，纽约也被视为世界外交的中心。

纽约属于世界级城市，人口众多。为了应对大量的人潮，纽约的公共运输大多为 24 小时营业。在纽约出行，交通方式首选地铁，纽约的地铁站有 468 个。

推荐的游玩景点有：帝国大厦、自由女神像、时代广场、第五大道、中央公园、大都会艺术博物馆、梅西百货公司。

[芝加哥] Chicago

芝加哥位于美国中西部，为美国第三大城市。由于芝加哥紧邻密歇根湖，绵延的湖岸线很适合租自行车漫游，乘船游览也是不错的方式。

推荐的游玩景点有：千禧公园、格兰特公园、海军码头、密歇根湖、芝加哥艺术馆。

[波士顿] Boston

波士顿位于大西洋沿岸，在美国的历史上有着举足轻重的地位，是美国最古老且具有历史文化价值的城市之一。因为紧邻海边，波士顿的海鲜非常有名，其中最著名的非波士顿龙虾莫属。

推荐的游玩景点有：波士顿公园、哈佛大学、三一教堂、自由之路、波士顿美术馆。

[西雅图] Seattle

大部分的人对西雅图的印象都来自电影《西雅图夜未眠》。位于太平洋沿岸的西雅图是文化与表演艺术中心。而知名连锁咖啡店"星巴克"第一家门店便是在西雅图开业的。

推荐的游玩景点有：太空针塔、西雅图美术馆、派克市场、口香糖墙、搭乘鸭子观光巴士。

[拉斯维加斯] City of Las Vegas

拉斯维加斯以博彩业而著名，拉斯维加斯大道上金碧辉煌的建筑，象征了拉斯维加斯的生命力，也因为博彩业的发展，带动了当地娱乐业的兴起。

[洛杉矶] City of Los Angeles

"Los Angeles"在西班牙语中的本意为"天使之城"。位于加州的洛杉矶，是仅次于纽约的美国第二大城市。电影产业的龙头"好莱坞"便位于此，虽然许多电影公司都已经迁移，但在星光大道上好莱坞明星的星章，便是电影产业曾在此蓬勃发展的证明。

推荐的游玩景点有：好莱坞大道、迪士尼乐园、环球影城、威尼斯海岸、圣塔莫尼卡湾、格里斐斯天文馆。

[旧金山] San Francisco

中文又称"三藩市"，而因为其多雾的天气，又被称为"雾城"。由于处在丘陵地上，因此市区内有许多直上直下的街道，成为旧金山独特的风景。

推荐的游玩景点有：金门大桥、金门公园、渔人码头、阿尔卡特拉斯岛（俗称：恶魔岛），也可搭乘路面缆车悠游于市区。

美国重要节日

复活节（Easter）
每年春分月圆后的第一个星期日。复活节兔与复活节彩蛋是此节日的代表，兔子象征生命力，而蛋象征初春的生机，一般会在蛋上绘制各种图案。在复活节当天，白宫也会举办滚彩蛋活动。

感恩节（Thanksgiving Day）
11月的第四个星期四。在感恩节，亲友们会团聚共进晚餐，而最传统、最重要的主菜即为火鸡，一般会在火鸡肚中塞满配料并且整只烘烤，用餐时则由男主人负责动刀切肉。美国总统在这一天会赦免一只火鸡。

万圣节（Halloween）
10月31日。到了这一天，小孩子都会变装、戴面具，上街敲门大喊"Trick or Treat!"来要糖果。而另一个代表万圣节的物品为南瓜灯笼（Jack O'Lantern），利用南瓜雕刻出怪物般的鬼脸，并在中间放置蜡烛。

圣诞节（Christmas）
12月25日，主要是为了庆祝耶稣诞生。如今圣诞节写卡片、送圣诞礼物已成为全球风行的习惯，而在美国，圣诞节也代表家庭团聚的日子，一般家庭会以圣诞灯及装饰布置圣诞树。

1月1日	新年 美国各州会举行极富地方色彩的庆祝活动。
7月4日	独立日 即为美国国庆，纪念美国于1776年7月4日发表《独立宣言》。
9月的第一个星期一	劳动节 以示对劳动者的尊重，当日放假一天。

常用提问说法

- 什么时候? **When?**
- 谁? **Who?**
- 哪里? **Where?**
- 为什么? **Why?**

常用的自我介绍说法

- 你来自哪里? **Where are you from?**
- 我来自中国。**I'm from China.**
- 你叫什么名字? **What's your name?**
- 我姓李。**My last name is Li.**
- 很高兴认识你。**Nice to meet you.**
- 很高兴认识你。(正式) **It's a pleasure to meet you.**

请求帮忙的旅游会话

你可以帮我吗？
Can you help me?

可以再请你说一次吗？
May I beg your pardon?

可以麻烦你说慢一点吗？
Would you mind speaking slower?

这里有会说中文的人吗？
Does anybody speak Chinese here?

能请你写在纸上吗？
Can you write on the paper, please?

我不（大）懂你的意思。
I don't understand what you mean.

能请你带我去吗？
Can you take me there, please?

可以请你帮忙吗？
Can you do me a favor?

出发前 | 机场相关 | 国外住宿 | 观光景点 | 异国美食 | 购物乐趣 | 国外交通 | 紧急状况

♪011

不可不知的旅游会话

不好意思,我要结账。
Excuse me, check out.

这个多少钱?
How much is it?

我想要买这个。
I want to buy this.

可以用信用卡(现金)结账吗?
Can I pay by credit card (in cash)?

现在有折扣吗?
Do you give a discount?

不好意思,我们只收现金。
Sorry, we only take cash.

我可以试穿吗?
May I try it on?

我可以尝尝吗?
May I have a taste of it?

你推荐哪一个?
Which one do you recommend?

请问你想要买这项产品吗?
Excuse me, do you want to buy this product?

好的。
Yes, please.

没问题。
No problem.

不用了。
No, thanks.

我考虑一下。
I will think it over.

请问有位子吗?
Excuse me, are there seats available?

我想要买饮料。
I'd like to buy some drinks.

我想要点餐。
I'm ready to order.

你可以点外带吗?
Would you mind ordering for to go?

一定要会的句型	适用状况
请给我 _____。 **Please give me _____.**	适用于任何想要索取物品的场合，例如：用餐、购物、车站、酒店、旅游资讯中心。
_____在哪里？ **Where is the way to _____?**	迷路时很实用的句型，只要在空格中填入想去的地点就可以了。
_____在哪里？ **Where is _____?**	不管是找商品，或是找地点、找服务人员，都可以使用这个句型，空格中可放想买的物品、想找的人。
你们有_____吗？ **Do you have _____?**	在商店找寻某项物品时，可能会花太多时间，可以询问店员，确定店里是否有此商品，确认有的话，便可再运用上一个"Where is _____?"的句型了。
我在找_____。 **I'm looking for _____.**	寻找地点、寻找物品、寻找想买的东西等情况，都可以使用这个句型。
_____多少钱？ **How much is _____?**	适用于任何询问价钱的情况，可以问商品的价格，也可以问车费，甚至是服务的价钱，空格中只要填入想询问的物品名称就可以了。
我可以_____吗？ **May I _____?**	不确定是否可以做某些事情（拍照、点餐、预约等）时，可以询问服务人员。
可以请你_____吗？ **Would you mind _____?**	需要他人协助时，可以使用这个句型，空格中可填入想请对方帮忙的事情。

Chapter 2
机场相关

出国前，首先要处理的是机票问题，如果觉得自己在网上订票太麻烦的话，也可以请旅行社代为订购。现在去某些国家可以免签证，省去办理签证的手续，但各个国家的规定不同，记得事先做好功课哦！

Hurry up!

走吧！出发去旅行！

买好机票，带着行李、护照，出发吧！

订机票

我想订一张飞往芝加哥的机票。	**I'm going to book one ticket to Chicago.**
飞往洛杉矶最早的航班是哪班？	What's the earliest flight to Los Angeles?
有早上出发的班机吗？	Do you have any flights in the morning?
飞机是降落在洛杉矶机场吗？	Is the plane going to land at the Los Angeles Airport?
现在订票有优惠吗？	Are there any discounts available now?
飞机几点出发？	**When will the plane depart?**
飞机几点降落？	**When will the plane land?**
可以请你解释订票流程吗？	Could you explain the procedure of booking tickets?
我需要在几号前完成开票呢？	What date shall I issue my ticket?
红眼航班会更便宜吗？	Is the night flight much cheaper?
机票多少钱？	**How much is the flight ticket?**

费用含燃油费吗？	Is the fuel tax included?
我的飞机餐想要素食餐。	I'm going to have an inflight meal for vegetarian diet.

柜台报到

你好，我要报到。	**Hello. Check in, please.**
请问是在这里报到吗？	**Excuse me, may I check in here?**
请问 ZE352 航班要到哪里报到？	Excuse me, where should I check in for ZE352?
请问国航的柜台在哪里？	Excuse me, where's the check-in counter for China Airlines?
CA692 开始报到了吗？	Does CA692 start to check in?
CX451 航班的旅客请到柜台报到。	Passengers for CX451, please check in at the check-in counter.
7：50 飞往旧金山的旅客请至柜台。	Passengers for San Francisco at 7:50, please go to the check-in counter.
你想要靠窗还是靠走道的位置？	Would you like a window seat or an aisle seat?
请给我靠窗（走道）的位子。	I'd like to have a window (an aisle) seat.

♪ 017

走吧！一起用英语去旅行！

麻烦给我你的护照。	May I see your passport?
护照在这里。	Here is my passport.
请问是李小姐吗？	Excuse me, are you Miss Li?
请将护照套取下。	Please take off the cover of the passport.
请在 9：45 前抵达 15 号登机门。	**Please arrive at Gate 15 by 9:45.**
您的登机门在 52 号。	Your boarding gate is 52.

行李托运

请问有要托运的行李吗？	**Do you have any luggage to check in?**
请将行李放到秤上。	Please put your luggage on the scale.
托运行李中有移动电源吗？	Is there any mobile power pack in the check-in luggage?
托运行李中不能有移动电源。	It's not allowed to put any mobile power pack in the check-in luggage.
托运行李只有一件吗？	Do you only have one piece of check-in luggage?

不好意思，你的行李超重了。	Excuse me, your luggage is overweight.
需要跟你索取行李超重费用。	We need to charge you the extra fee of the overweight luggage.
要确保你的行李能通过X光机。	Make sure that your luggage passes the X-ray machine.
这是你的随身行李吗？	Is this your carry-on luggage?

安全检查

随身行李里不能有尖锐物品。	Sharp objects are not allowed to be put into the carry-on luggage.
不能携带超过100ml的液体。	Over 100ml liquid is not allowed to carry.
麻烦请通过金属探测器。	Please go through the metal detector gate.
请摘下手表，再走一次。	Please take off your watch, and walk through once again.
包与大衣请放在不同的篮子里。	Please put the bag and the coat into different baskets.
你需要进行搜身检查。	You have to submit to a body search.

麻烦站直,并双手平举。	Please stand straight and hands flat.
要麻烦你把口袋里的硬币拿出来。	Please take out your coins in your pockets.
麻烦丢掉矿泉水瓶。	Please throw away the mineral water.
抱歉,自拍杆不能带上飞机。	Sorry, the selfie stick is not allowed to be taken on the plane.

免税店

每人可带一条烟入境。	**Everyone is allowed to bring a carton of cigarettes to enter the country.**
过海关时,每人只能携带一瓶酒。	**When going through the Customs, everyone can bring just one bottle of wine.**
我们可以买高粱酒给外国友人。	We can buy Kaoliang for our foreign friends.
需要帮忙吗?	Can I help you?
我想要找这个牌子的香烟。	I'd like to look for this brand of cigarettes.
这是机场超值装吗?	Is this the great deal in the airport?

| 请问你们卖伏特加吗？ | Excuse me, do you sell vodka? |
| 机场里面有蔻依的专卖店吗？ | Is there Chloé Specialty Store in the airport? |

候机室

请问 C50 的登机门在哪里？	Excuse me, where's the boarding gate of C50?
↓	
沿着走廊直走，在蔻驰专卖店的对面。	Walk along this hallway, it's opposite the COACH Store.

请问我要怎么去第二航站楼呢？	How can I go to Terminal 2?
↓	
你需要搭乘接驳巴士前往。	You need to take the shuttle bus to get there.

| 我们需要从闸口搭乘接驳巴士登机吗？ | Should we transfer to take the shuttle bus from the gate to board on the plane? |

| 受到暴风雪的影响，机场即将关闭，所有班机将延迟起飞。 | Due to the snow storm, the airport will be closed. All the flights will be delayed to take off. |

出发前

机场相关

国外住宿

观光景点

异国美食

购物乐趣

国外交通

紧急状况

♪ 021

句型

一张去_____的机票。

A ticket to _____ .

[城市]

Orlando
[ɔː'lændəʊ]
奥兰多

San Francisco
[ˌsænfrənˈsɪskəʊ]
旧金山

New York
['njuː 'jɔːk]
纽约

Boston
['bɒstən]
波士顿

Chicago
[ʃɪ'kɑːgəʊ]
芝加哥

Los Angeles
[lɔsˈændʒləs]
洛杉矶

[机场]

John F. Kennedy International Airport
肯尼迪国际机场

Los Angeles International Airport
洛杉矶国际机场

Orlando International Airport
奥兰多国际机场

O'Hare International Airport
奥黑尔国际机场

请问_____在哪里？

Excuse me, where is (the) _____ ?

check-in counter
['tʃekɪn 'kaʊntə]
报到柜台

boarding gate
['bɔːdɪŋ geɪt]
登机门

security point
[sɪ'kjʊərəti pɔɪnt]
安检处

shuttle bus
['ʃʌtl bʌs]
接驳车

| **duty-free shop** [ˌdjuːti ˈfriː ʃɒp] 免税店 | **information counter** [ˌɪnfəˈmeɪʃn ˈkaʊntə] 服务台 | **toilet** [ˈtɔɪlət] 厕所 | **food court** [fuːd kɔːt] 美食街 |

出发前

机场相关

| **VIP room** [ˌviː aɪ ˈpiː ruːm] VIP 休息室 | **water fountain** [ˈwɔːtə faʊntən] 饮水机 | **vending machine** [ˈvendɪŋ məʃiːn] 贩卖机 | **terminal** [ˈtɜːmɪnl] 航站楼 |

国外住宿

观光景点

禁止携带_____。

No _____ allowed.

| | | **scissors** [ˈsɪzəz] 剪刀 | **gun** [ɡʌn] 枪 |

异国美食

| **club** [klʌb] 棍棒 | **Swiss army knife** [ˌswɪs ˈɑːmi naɪf] 瑞士刀 | | |

购物乐趣

| **100ml liquid** [ˈlɪkwɪd] 100ml 的液体 | **baseball bat** [ˈbeɪsbɔːl bæt] 棒球棒 | **lighter** [ˈlaɪtə] 打火机 | **electric baton** [ɪˈlektrɪk ˈbætɒn] 电击棒 |

国外交通

紧急状况

单词

[行李]

check-in luggage
[tʃek ɪn 'lʌɡɪdʒ]
托运行李

carry-on luggage
['kæri ɒn 'lʌɡɪdʒ]
随身行李

clothes
[kləʊdz]
衣物

baggage tag
['bæɡɪdʒ tæɡ]
行李挂牌

toiletry
['tɔɪlɪtrɪ]
盥洗用品

cosmetics
[kɒz'metɪks]
化妆品

individual drugs
[ˌɪndɪ'vɪdʒuəl drʌɡz]
个人药品

underwear
['ʌndəweə]
内衣

cellphone
['selfəʊn]
手机

mobile power pack
['məʊbaɪl 'paʊə pæk]
移动电源

battery charger
['bætri 'tʃɑːdʒə]
充电器

camera
['kæmərə]
相机

cash
[kæʃ]
现金

credit card
['kredɪt kɑːd]
信用卡

traveling book
['trævlɪŋ bʊk]
旅游书

selfie stick
['selfi stɪk]
自拍杆

schedule
['skedʒuːl]
行程表

camera tripod
['kæmərə 'traɪpɒd]
相机三脚架

♪ 024

[机场]

sign board
[saɪn bɔːd]
指示牌

luggage cart
[ˈlʌɡɪdʒ kɑːt]
行李推车

currency counter
[ˈkʌrənsi ˈkaʊntə]
外币柜台

insurance counter
[ɪnˈʃʊərəns ˈkaʊntə]
保险柜台

free WIFI
[friː ˈwaɪ faɪ]
免费 WIFI

airport hall
[ˈeəpɔːt hɔːl]
机场大厅

traveler
[ˈtrævələ]
旅客

airport bus
[ˈeəpɔːt bʌs]
机场巴士

[机场人员]

pilot
[ˈpaɪlət]
机师

stewardess
[ˌstjuːəˈdes]
空姐

[机票资讯]

customs officer
[ˈkʌstəmz ˈɒfɪsə]
海关人员

flight ticket
[flaɪt ˈtɪkɪt]
机票

departure
[dɪˈpɑːtʃə]
出发地

departure time
[dɪˈpɑːtʃə taɪm]
出发时间

boarding gate
[ˈbɔːdɪŋ ɡeɪt]
登机门

flight
[flaɪt]
航班

arrival
[əˈraɪvl]
抵达地

arrival time
[əˈraɪvl taɪm]
抵达时间

boarding time
[ˈbɔːdɪŋ taɪm]
登机时间

seat
[siːt]
座位

出发前 | 机场相关 | 国外住宿 | 观光景点 | 异国美食 | 购物乐趣 | 国外交通 | 紧急状况

顺利抵达目的地了！

搭上飞机，放松心情，几个小时后就到了。

▌准备登机

CX510 将在 10 分钟后开始登机。	**CX510 is going to start to board in ten minutes.**
请带小孩的旅客先行登机。	**Passengers with kids are first to board, please.**
现在开放前排座位的旅客登机。	It's now time for the passengers in the forward to board.
请出示你的登机证及护照。	Please show me your boarding pass and passport.
这是 HA628 的最后一次登机广播。	It's the last boarding announcement for HA628.
欢迎搭乘西北航空。	Welcome to aboard Northwest Airlines.

▌飞机服务

座位 45C 请直走后右转。	Seat 45C is to go straight and then make a right turn.
请问有空位可以让我换一下吗？	Excuse me, is there any available seat to change for me?

♪ 026

麻烦请多给我一条毛毯和枕头。	**Please give me one more blanket and pillow.**
请问有报纸吗？	Is there any newspaper?
麻烦请系好安全带。	**Please fasten your seat belt.**
飞机滑行时请勿走动。	Please do not walk while the airplane is taxiing.
行李请放到舱顶置物柜。	Please put your luggage in the overhead compartment.
麻烦请将椅背竖直。	**Please upright your chair.**
我的耳机没有声音。	There's no sound of my headphone.
我想要购买机上的免税品。	I'd like to buy some in-flight duty-free items.

▎飞机餐点

你好，这是你的素食餐。	Hello, this is your vegetarian diet.
请问要鸡肉饭还是猪肉面？	Excuse me, would you like chicken rice or pork noodles?
鸡肉饭，谢谢。	Chicken rice, please.

♪ 027

请问要喝什么饮料？	Would you like something to drink?
苹果汁，谢谢。	Apple juice, please.
我想要一杯可乐。	I'd like a cup of Coke.
我可以点一杯红酒吗？	May I have a glass of red wine?
可以请你给我一杯温水吗？	**Would you mind giving me a cup of warm water?**
你的咖啡需要糖或奶精吗？	Do you need any sugar or coffee mate for your coffee?

入境

请填写入境卡。	**Please fill in the disembarkation card.**
请问入境卡在哪里拿？	Excuse me, where can I get the disembarkation card?
请问你来美国的目的是什么？	What's your purpose to America?
我是来旅游的（出差的）。	I'm here to go sightseeing (on business).
麻烦请在这里排队。	Please line up here.

请问你在美国住宿的酒店?	Which hotel will you stay at in America?
芝加哥的美国长住酒店。	The Extended Stay America Hotel in Chicago.
请问你预计停留几天?	How many days will you stay?
预计停留 5 天。	I will stay for five days.

领取行李

我不知道要去哪里领行李。	I don't know where to get my luggage.
EX578 的行李在 10 号行李转盘。	**The luggage of EX578 is on the Carousel 10.**
行李似乎还没有出来。	The luggage seems to be not out.
我的行李不见了。	My luggage is gone.
怎么办?我找不到我的行李。	I can't find my luggage. What should I do?
糟糕!我的行李箱裂开了!	Whoops! My baggage tore apart!

♪ 029

走吧！一起用英语去旅行！

我的行李箱被摔坏了！	My luggage was broken!
要去哪里看行李转盘的信息呢？	Where can I check the information of baggage carousel?
手扶梯下方有电子布告栏。	There's an electric bulletin below the escalator.
可以帮我找一辆行李推车吗？	Could you help me to get a luggage cart?

▎离开机场

我要去哪里买蓝线的票？	Where can I buy the blue line ticket?
去迪文森的公交站牌在哪里呢？	Where's the bus stop to Division?
下班往市区的接驳车何时发车？	When does the next shuttle bus to downtown start?
有哪些车可以到芝加哥市区呢？	What buses can lead to Chicago downtown?
请问从星辰酒店到机场的接驳车要去哪里搭乘？	Excuse me, where can I take the shuttle bus from the Star Hotel to the airport?

这条路线的公交车可以到我们的酒店吗？	Does this route of the bus lead to our hotel?
你建议我们坐公交还是出租车？	Do you recommend us to take the bus or the taxi?
虽然搭乘公交的时间比较久，但比较划算。	It's worth it although it will take much longer to take the bus.
我们错过了想要搭乘的那辆公交。	We missed that bus which we wanted to take.
我可以在这里买往返票吗？	Can I buy the round-trip ticket here?

[机场常见地点]

Check-in counter
[ˈtʃekɪn ˈkaʊntə]
自助报到机

tax refund counter
[tæks riːfʌnd ˈkaʊntə]
退税柜台

currency exchange counter
[ˈkʌrənsɪ ɪksˈtʃeɪndʒ ˈkaʊntə]
外币兑换柜台

telecom counter
[ˈtelɪkɔm ˈkaʊntə]
电信公司柜台

ticket vending machine
[ˈtɪkɪt ˈvendɪŋ məˈʃiːn]
自动售票机

airport sky train
[ˈeəpɔːt skaɪ treɪn]
航站联结电车

a departure lounge
[ə dɪˈpɑːtʃə laʊndʒ]
候机室

e-Gate
[ˈiːgeɪt]
自动通关机

luggage claim area
[ˈlʌgɪdʒ kleɪm ˈeərɪə]
提领行李处

traveling information center
[ˈtrævəɪŋ ɪnfəˈmeɪʃn ˈsenə]
旅游资讯中心

♪ 031

单词

[飞机上]

seat
[siːt]
座位

window seat
[ˈwɪndəʊ siːt]
靠窗座位

first class
[fɜːst klɑːs]
头等舱

boarding bridge
[ˈbɔːdɪŋ brɪdʒ]
登机桥

aisle seat
[aɪl siːt]
靠走道座位

economy class
[ɪˈkɒnəmi klɑːs]
经济舱

blanket
[ˈblæŋkɪt]
毛毯

cushion
[ˈkʊʃn]
靠枕

headphone
[ˈhedfəʊn]
耳机

duty free catalog
[ˈdjuːti friː ˈkætəlɒg]
免税品目录

program schedule
[ˈprəʊgræm ˈskedʒuːl]
节目表

life vest
[laɪf vest]
救生衣

oxygen mask
[ˈɒksɪdʒən mɑːsk]
氧气罩

emergency exit
[ɪˈmɜːdʒənsi ˈeksɪt]
紧急出口

screen
[skriːn]
荧幕

table
[ˈteɪbl]
桌子

[餐点饮料]

Coke
[kəʊk]
可乐

Sprite
[spraɪt]
雪碧

soda
[ˈsəʊdə]
汽水

drinks
[drɪŋks]
饮料

juice [dʒu:s] 果汁	**apple juice** [ˈæpl dʒu:s] 苹果汁	**orange juice** [ˈɒrɪndʒ dʒu:s] 橙汁	**hot tea** [hɒt ti:] 热茶	出发前

机场相关

coffee [ˈkɒfi] 咖啡	**red wine** [ˌred ˈwaɪn] 红酒	**white wine** [ˌwaɪt ˈwaɪn] 白酒	**champagne** [ʃæmˈpeɪn] 香槟

国外住宿

ice cube [ˈaɪs kju:b] 冰块

观光景点

[机场]	**customs** [ˈkʌstəmz] 海关	**passport** [ˈpɑ:spɔ:t] 护照	**passport cover** [ˈpɑ:spɔ:t ˈkʌvə] 护照套

各国美食

disembarkation card [dɪsˌembɑ:ˈkeɪʃn kɑ:d] 入境卡	**declaration form** [ˌdekləˈreɪʃn fɔ:m] 申报单		**transfer** v [trænsˈfɜ:] n [ˈtrænsfɜ:] 转机

购物乐趣

escalator [ˈeskəleɪtə] 手扶梯	**elevator** [ˈelɪveɪtə] 电梯	**arrival** [əˈraɪvl] 入境	**boarding area** [ˈbɔ:dɪŋ ˌeərɪə] 登机区

国外交通

		departure [dɪˈpɑ:tʃə] 出境	**bus stand** [bʌs stænd] 公交车搭乘处

紧急状况

♪ 033

美国签证介绍

事先申请,取得授权!

申请流程如下:

填写表格 → 准备材料 → 预约付款 → 使馆面签

填写表格

至 https://ceac.state.gov/genniv/default.aspx 在线填写 DS-160 非移民签证申请表。表格中有一项要求用母语填写姓名,可使用汉字填写名字,除此之外,所有内容必须用英语填写。

准备材料

1. 有效因私护照,护照末页有本人签名。
2. 2 张 2 英寸彩色免冠照片,身份证、工作证、结婚证、户口本复印件,单位简介,工作名片 4 张,公司出具的在职证明,报名表,银行近半年银行流水单证明。

付款预约

1. 支付签证费,支付完成后,打印收据编号并妥善保管。如预约时不能提供收据编号,将无法进行预约。
2. 向美国使馆预约面签时间,要提供的材料、签证费收据号、护照号码、身份证号,DS-160 表的编号。

使馆面签

按照约定时间到美国大使馆进行面签,请随身携带预约单打印件、DS-160 确认页打印件,一张近 6 个月的照片,护照。

美国签证类型 非移民签证

签证类别	目的与签证内容
A	外交人员及外国政府官员
A1-2、G1-4、NATO1-6	在美国的签证续签 - A、G 及 NATO
A-2、NATO1-6	驻美国外国军事人员
B-1	商务访客
B-2	求医访客；旅游、度假、娱乐访客
BCC	边境出入境卡：墨西哥
C	过境美国
D	船员或机组人员（于美国境内在船只或航班上服务）
F-1	学生——一般学院及语言学校学生
F-2	学生家属——F-1 持有人的眷属
I	媒体代表（媒体、新闻工作者）
R	宗教工作者

美国签证类型 移民签证

- **亲属移民**

  不受限额限制：美国已成年公民的父母、配偶或未成年子女。

  受到限额限制：持有永久居留权的配偶或子女；美国公民的已成年子女和兄弟姐妹。

- **就业移民**：优先工作者；专业人才；专业雇员；特殊移民；投资人士

美国主要机场

对于美国来说,因为国土辽阔,航空是非常重要的交通方式,再加上美国为发达国家,前往观光、商务、就学的国外人士也不少。每年对于全世界最繁忙机场的调查,许多美国机场都名列前茅。

美国东岸主要机场

纽约－肯尼迪国际机场
(IATA 机场代码:**JFK**)

迈阿密－迈阿密国际机场
(IATA 机场代码:**MIA**)

亚特兰大－哈茨菲尔德－杰克逊机场
(IATA 机场代码:**ATL**)

弗吉尼亚州－华盛顿杜勒斯国际机场
(IATA 机场代码:**IAD**)

★ 华盛顿杜勒斯国际机场

美国西岸主要机场

洛杉矶－洛杉矶国际机场
(IATA 机场代码:**LAX**)

西雅图－塔科马国际机场
(IATA 机场代码:**SEA**)

拉斯维加斯－麦卡伦国际机场
(IATA 机场代码:**LAS**)

丹佛市－丹佛国际机场
(IATA 机场代码:**DEN**)

★ 丹佛国际机场

Chapter 3 国外住宿

处理完机票,接下来就要来面对住宿的问题。根据游玩的行程,选择交通方便的投宿地点,最好在地铁站附近,可以省下许多交通时间。如果想要在酒店放松,星级酒店或度假村是不错的选择。

Relax and enjoy...

先去酒店办理入住吧！

先到酒店放个行李，休息后再整装出发。

订房

我想要订房。	**I'd like to book a room.**
6月1日到6月5日有空的双人房一间吗？	Is there a double room available from June 1st to June 5th?
今天晚上还有空房吗？	Is there any available room tonight?
我想要无烟房。	I'd like a non-smoking room.
我想要吸烟房。	I'd like a smoking room.
房间可以加床吗？	May I have an extra bed in my room?
单人房多少钱？	**How much is for a single room?**
我需要先支付订金吗？	Do I need to prepay for the deposit?
请问有早餐吗？	**Is breakfast included?**
请问从机场有接驳车可搭乘吗？	Is there any shuttle bus from the airport?

♪ 038

什么时候入住和退房？	When is for check in and check out?

登记入住

请问办理入住手续的柜台在哪里？	Excuse me, where is the check-in counter?
我想要登记入住。	I'd like to check in.
你好，我有订房。	Hi, I've booked a room.
我的订房编号是150322001。	My reservation number is 150322001.
这间是双人房吗？	Is this a double room?
有会说中文的服务人员吗？	Does any staff speak Chinese?
我可以先将行李寄放在柜台吗？	Can I put my luggage at the luggage counter first?
我可以提早入住房间吗？	Can I check in earlier?

走吧！一起用英语去旅行！

请问最晚何时要登记入住？	Excuse me, when is the latest to check in?
请问我可以延迟退房吗？	Excuse me, can I check out later?
麻烦请填写这张表格并签名。	Please fill out this form and sign your name here.
麻烦请出示你的护照及信用卡。	Please show me your passport and your credit card.
好的，在这里。	Sure, here they are.

房间介绍

你订的是一间商务套房，住2晚。	You've booked a business suite for two nights.
这是你的房卡，638号房。	**Here is your room card, Room 638.**
你的房间在8楼，816号房。	**Your room is on the eighth floor, Room 816.**
两间房间都在6楼，624和625号房。	Two rooms are both on the sixth floor, Room 624 and Room 625.
房间面对山景，景观漂亮。	The room faces the mountainous scenery, which is very beautiful.

前面右转即可搭电梯上楼。	Turn right in front and you can take the elevator to go upstairs.
制冰机在走道两侧,可自行取用。	Ice makers are on both sides of the aisle. Please be free to take them.

早餐介绍

这是这几天的早餐券。	**Here are breakfast vouchers for these days.**
请问早餐几点钟供应?	Excuse me, when is the breakfast service?
↓ 早餐供应时间为7点到9点半。	Breakfast service is from 7 o'clock to half past 9.
请问在哪里吃早餐呢?	Excuse me, where are we going to have breakfast?
↓ 在一楼餐厅。	At the restaurant on the first floor.
将早餐券交给服务人员即可。	Give the breakfast voucher to the staff.

询问服务

请问提供 Wi-Fi 吗?	**Do you provide Wi-Fi service?**

走吧！一起用英语去旅行！

酒店大厅（房间）有免费 Wi-Fi 吗？	Is there any free Wi-Fi in the lobby (in the room)?
请问 Wi-Fi 的密码是多少？	Excuse me, what's the password of Wi-Fi?
Wi-Fi 的密码为 536，你的房号。	The Wi-Fi password is 536, your room number.
请问有代寄明信片的服务吗？	Excuse me, do you have the service to send post cards?
请问有我的包裹吗？	Excuse me, is there my package?
请问可以代订公交车票吗？	**Excuse me, can you help me to book the bus tickets?**
请问有这个地区的地图吗？	Excuse me, do you have the map of this area?
如果我想要看百老汇的表演，可以帮我购票吗？	If I want to see the Broadway Show, could you help me to buy tickets?
请问有推荐的旅游行程吗？	Do you recommend any traveling itineraries?
你们提供按摩服务吗？	Do you offer massage service?

酒店与周围环境

住宿的旅客都可以免费使用游泳池吗？	Is it free for the visitors of the hotel to use the swimming pool?
健身房什么时间开放？	When is it open for the fitness center?
酒店周边有什么推荐的景点吗？	**Do you recommend any scenic spots around the hotel?**
请问这里离时代广场有多远？	Excuse me, how far is Times Square from here?
我们距离时代广场有两个街区远。	There are two blocks far away from Times Square.
如果我想要去当代美术馆，走路可以到吗？	If I want to go to Contemporary Art Museum, can I walk there?
这个时间，我可以去哪里买吃的呢？	Where can I grab something to eat during this period?
转角有家热狗摊很好吃，可以试试。	There's a hot dog stand around the corner. It's delicious, and you can try it.

♪ 043

句型

一间_____。
A _____.

| **single room** ['sɪŋgl ruːm] 单人房 | **double room** ['dʌbl ruːm] 双人房 |

quad [kwɒd] 四人房

business suite ['bɪznəs swiːt] 商务套房

smoking room ['sməʊkɪŋ ruːm] 吸烟房

non-smoking room [,nɒn 'sməʊkɪŋ ruːm] 无烟房

family suite ['fæməli swiːt] 家庭套房

view suite [vjuː swiːt] 景观套房

请问房间里有_____吗？
Is there (a / an) _____ in the room?

television ['telɪvɪʒn] 电视

refrigerator [rɪ'frɪdʒəreɪtə] 冰箱

iron [,aɪən] 熨斗

coffer ['kɒfə] 保险箱

toiletry ['tɔɪlɪtrɪ] 盥洗用品

hair dryer [heə 'draɪə] 吹风机

French windows [,frentʃ 'wɪndəʊz] 落地窗

balcony ['bælkəni] 阳台

single bed [,sɪŋgl 'bed] 单人床

double bed ['dʌbl 'bed] 双人床

electric kettle
[ɪˈlektrɪk ˈketl]
电热水壶

mug
[mʌg]
马克杯

hanger
[ˈhæŋə]
衣架

wardrobe
[ˈwɔːdrəub]
衣柜

请问酒店有_____吗？

Excuse me, is there (a / an)_____ in the hotel?

restaurant
[ˈrestrɒnt]
餐厅

ball room
[bɔːl ruːm]
宴会厅

conference
[ˈkɒnfərəns]
会议室

fitness center
[ˈfɪtnəs sentə]
健身房

SPA center
[spɑː ˈsentə]
SPA 馆

convenience store
[kənˈviːnɪəns stɔː(r)]
便利店

vending machine
[ˈvendɪŋ məʃiːn]
售卖机

shuttle bus
[ˈʃʌtl bʌs]
接驳巴士

laundromat
[ˈlɔːndrəmæt]
投币式自助洗衣店

tour guide
[tʊə gaɪd]
导游

taxi service
[ˈtæksi ˈsɜːvɪs]
叫车服务

city map
[ˈsɪti mæp]
市区地图

出发前 | 机场相关 | 国外住宿 | 观光景点 | 异国美食 | 购物乐趣 | 国外交通 | 紧急状况

单词

[投宿地点]

business hotel	resort	capsule hotel
['bɪznəs həʊ'tel]	[rɪ'zɔːt]	['kæpsjuːl həʊ'tel]
商务旅馆	度假村	胶囊旅馆

hotel	five-star hotel	B & B	youth hostel
[həʊ'tel]	['faɪv staː(r) həʊ'tel]	[biː ənd biː]	['juːθ hɒstl]
旅馆	五星级酒店	民宿	青年旅社

[酒店人员]

receptionist [rɪ'sepʃənɪst] 接待人员

doorman ['dɔːmən] 门房

porter ['pɔːtə] 行李员

traveler ['trævləə] 旅客

[房间设备]

bed [bed] 床铺

table ['teɪbl] 桌子

chair [tʃeə] 椅子

room [ruːm] 房间

light [laɪt] 电灯

lamp [læmp] 桌灯

air conditioner [eə kən'dɪʃənə] 空调

bedside cupboard ['bedsaɪd 'kʌbəd] 床头柜

dehumidifier [diːhjuː'mɪdɪfaɪə] 除湿机

drawer [drɔː] 抽屉

♪ 046

[盥洗用品]

bathroom ['bɑːθruːm] 浴室	**bathtub** ['bɑːθtʌb] 浴缸	**toilet** ['tɔɪlət] 马桶	**faucet** ['fɔːsɪt] 水龙头

showerhead ['ʃaʊəhed] 莲蓬头	**shower curtain** ['ʃaʊə 'kɜːtn] 浴帘		**soap** [səʊp] 香皂

| | **door** [dɔː] 门 | **tooth mug** [tuːθ mʌg] 漱口杯 | |

shower shampoo ['ʃaʊə ʃæm'puː] 沐浴乳	**hair shampoo** [heə ʃæm'puː] 洗发乳	**hair conditioner** [heə kən'dɪʃənə] 润发乳	**toothbrush & toothpaste** ['tuːθbrʌʃ ənd 'tuːθpeɪst] 牙刷与牙膏

brush [brʌʃ] 梳子	**razor** ['reɪzə] 剃须刀	**shower cap** ['ʃaʊə kæp] 浴帽	**Q-tip** ['kjuː tɪp] 棉花棒

cotton pad ['kɒtn pæd] 化妆棉

出发前 | 机场相关 | 国外住宿 | 观光景点 | 异国美食 | 购物乐趣 | 国外交通 | 紧急状况

♪ 047

美国住宿介绍

在美国住宿，你可以有以下各种选择：

酒店

酒店是一般旅客会选择投宿的地点，主要是因为具备住宿所需的各项设备，酒店还会提供客房服务、洗衣服务等，也可以在柜台询问服务人员各种旅游、票券资讯。

酒店的住宿价格根据品质、所在位置、提供的服务而定，一般会以星级评比来为酒店分级，星级越高，代表酒店的规模越大、服务越好，价钱也越高，但因为每个国家的风俗民情不同，所以目前星级评比并没有统一的标准。因此在决定要投宿的酒店之前，可以多上网搜寻网友分享的住宿经验。

酒店之所以有名，除了大家的推荐之外，也可能因为其独特性而被大家所知。例如：曾举办过重要的会议、与流行音乐或电影有关、有特殊知名的餐点等。

世界知名酒店集团

◆ 希尔顿国际酒店集团（Hilton Worldwide Holdings Inc.）
◆ 万豪国际酒店集团公司（Marriott International）
◆ 洲际国际酒店集团（Intercontinental Hotels Group）
◆ 雅高集团（Accor Hotels）

汽车旅馆

汽车旅馆（motel）多位于高速公路附近或是离城镇较远的公路旁，主要的投宿者是以汽车或摩托车代步的旅客。

多数汽车旅馆的停车位和房间是相连的，可能是在门前设立停车位，或是一楼为车库、二楼为房间的独门独户。但由于这样的设置会使得房间数量无法提升，所以也有像照片中一样是多层楼的房间，停车场统一在建筑物附近。

青年旅社

出国旅行，通常会在交通、住宿上花费最多，所以有些旅客会选择投宿青年旅社。青年旅社强调自助、实惠，大多是以多人房间为主，并有卫浴间、游戏室、交谊厅、厨房等公共空间，让旅客们共享空间并进行交流。

多数的青年旅社对投宿者并没有限制，投宿者以自助旅行者和背包客（backpacker）为主。青年旅社通常会设立在热门景点或是市中心，而设施说明一般会以英文与当地语言为主，以应对世界各地游客的需求。

退房！往下个地点前进！

以酒店为中心，玩遍附近景点后再移动吧！

客房服务

你好，这里是前台。	Hello, this is the front desk.
这里是 523 号房，想叫客房服务。	This is room number 523. I'd like the room service.
请问需要什么服务呢？	Excuse me, what can I do for you?
麻烦多送一条浴巾给我。	Please send me one more towel.
我需要多一条毛毯。	I need one more blanket.
可以多给我一个枕头吗？	May I have one more pillow?
我想要点一份鲜虾咖喱饭。	I'd like to order the shrimp curry rice.
麻烦尽快帮我送餐。	Please send my meal as soon as possible.
好的，马上帮你处理。	Sure. I'll do it for you right away.
谢谢你的帮忙。	Thanks for your help.

麻烦明天早上9点叫我起床。	I'd like a wake-up call at nine o'clock tomorrow.
好的，没有问题。	Okay, no problem.
你好，客房服务。	Hello, this is room service.

▍寻求帮忙

房间的电视无法看。	**There are some problems with my TV in the room.**
浴室的电灯坏了。	The light is out of work in the bathroom.
排水口堵住了。	The drain is stuck.
马桶塞住了。	The toilet is clogged.
Wi-Fi无法连线。	Wi-Fi can't be connected.
有线网络无法使用。	Cabled Net can't be used.
水龙头没有热水。	There's no hot water from the faucet.
我被锁在房间外面。	**I am locked out of the room.**

走吧！一起用英语去旅行！

我把房卡放在房间里了。	**I left the room key (card) in the room.**
空调温度无法调节。	The temperature of the air conditioner can't be adjusted.
可以请你帮忙吗？	Excuse me, could you do me a favor, please?
我忘记房间保险箱的密码了。	I forgot the password of the safety box in the room.
请问可以借变压器吗？	**Excuse me, may I borrow a transformer, please?**
请问有延长线可以借用吗？	Excuse me, may I borrow an extension cord?
请问可以借转接头吗？	Excuse me, may I borrow an adapter?

赞美及抱怨

谢谢你们贴心的服务。	Thanks for your nice service.
房间的景观很漂亮。	The view of the room is very beautiful.
在这里住宿很开心。	Staying here is very happy.

谢谢你们对我们的照顾。	I appreciate that you take care of us.
为您服务是我们的荣幸。	It's our pleasure at your services.
住在这里比住在家里还要舒服。	Staying here is much more comfortable than living at home.
希望下次还有机会为您服务。	I would be glad at your services next time.
会的,我会找时间再来住的。	No problem, I will come here once again.
因为隔壁房客很吵,所以我没睡好。	I didn't sleep well because the next door neighbor was noisy.
棉被与枕头有霉味。	There's mildew smell of the comforter and pillow.
水龙头的水忽冷忽热的。	The water from the tap is sometimes cold and sometimes hot.
空调的温度似乎无法调节。	It seems that I can't adjust the temperature of the air conditioner.
灯泡一闪一闪的,让我的眼睛不舒服。	The bulb gleamed that it was uncomfortable for my eyes.

♪ 053

我的房间有股食物馊掉的味道。	There's mold smell of food in my room.

▎办理退房

你好，我要退房。	**Hello, I'd like to check out.**
麻烦尽快帮我办理退房，谢谢。	Please do me a favor to check out immediately. Thank you so much.
326号房要退房。	**Room number 326 is going to check out.**
不好意思，账单金额有点问题。	Excuse me. There's something wrong with the amount of the bill.
我没有点客房服务。	I didn't have the room service.
请问要刷卡还是付现？	Excuse me, would you like to pay by / with credit card or pay in cash?
我想用现金结账。	I'd like to pay in cash.
请问我可以多住一天吗？	Excuse me, may I stay for one more night?
不好意思，没有空房了。	Sorry, there's no vacancy room.

遗忘物品

我把手机忘在房间了。	I left my cellphone in the room.
请问有没有在房间发现一对耳环？	Excuse me, do you find a pair of earrings in the room?
我好像把名片放在桌上了。	It seemed that I put the name card on the table.
有没有在衣柜发现一顶帽子？	Do you find a hat in the closet?
我的大衣不见了，请问有人捡到吗？	I lost my coat. Did anybody pick it up?

特殊要求

请问我可以晚一个小时退房吗？	Excuse me, can I postpone to check out for one hour?
我可以先退房，但寄放行李在这里吗？	May I check out first, but put my luggage here?
寄放行李需要额外收费吗？	Do you charge extra fee if I put my luggage temporarily?
寄放行李是免费的，请不要担心。	It's free to put the baggage temporarily. Don't worry.

♪ 055

句型

麻烦请给我_____。
Please give me a (an) _____.

comforter
['kʌmfətə]
棉被

pillow
['pɪləʊ]
枕头

towel
['taʊəl]
毛巾

bath towel
[bɑːθ 'taʊəl]
浴巾

blow dryer
[bləʊ 'draɪə]
吹风机

adapter
[ə'dæptə]
转接器

extension cord
[ɪk'stenʃn kɔːd]
延长线

ash tray
[æʃ treɪ]
烟灰缸

请问可以将_____寄放在前台吗？

Excuse me, may I put the _____ at the front desk?

luggage
['lʌgɪdʒ]
行李

package
['pækɪdʒ]
包裹

valuable item
['væljuəbl 'aɪtəm]
贵重物品

frozen food
['frəʊzn fuːd]
需冷冻的食物

[费用]

free [fri:] 免费

discount ['dɪskaʊnt] 打折

expense tax [ɪk'spens tæks] 消费税

fee [fi:] 费用

charge [tʃɑ:dʒ] 收费

extra fee ['ekstrə fi:] 额外费用

service fee ['sɜ:vɪs fi:] 服务费

room charge [ru:m tʃɑ:dʒ] 房间费用

parking fee ['pɑ:kɪŋ fi:] 停车费用

the cost of a meal [ðə kɒst əv ə mi:l] 吃饭花费

room service fee [ru:m 'sɜ:vɪs fi:] 客房服务费用

[票券]

room key [ru:m ki:] 房卡

parking card ['pɑ:kɪŋ kɑ:d] 停车卡

breakfast voucher ['brekfəst 'vaʊtʃə] 早餐券

voucher ['vaʊtʃə] 优惠券

pass [pɑ:s] 乘车券

[酒店外部]

taxi stand ['tæksi stænd] 出租车停靠站

bus stop ['bʌs stɒp] 公交车站

ticket ['tɪkɪt] 门票

street [stri:t] 马路

出发前 | 机场相关 | 国外住宿 | 观光景点 | 异国美食 | 购物乐趣 | 国外交通 | 紧急状况

♪ 057

各种投宿方式

不同的住宿方式会为旅行增添不同的风味!

酒店订房

青年旅社

沙发客

上网注册成为会员,可以在自己家招待旅行者,也可以在各地入住当地会员的家。

食宿交换

住宿者以帮忙处理寄宿家庭的家务等劳动换取免费的食宿。

Chapter 4 观光景点

用英语走遍世界,自然不能错过各大景点,不管是"都市"路线,或是"自然"路线,只要玩得开心就好了。但如果想要玩得尽兴,在安排行程上就要留意路线的顺畅度,避免花太多时间与金钱在来往的交通上。

I'm the Queen of the World!

体验人文风土民情!

出国一定要去的景点,绝对不能错过。

▍游客服务中心

游客服务中心在哪里?	Where is the visitors center?
在车站的二楼。	It's on the second floor of the station.
顺着标识走就可以找到了。	Just follow the sign and you can find it.
请问有免费地图可以领取吗?	**Excuse me, are there any free maps to get?**
我可以拿一份观光导览手册吗?	**Can I take a travel guide?**
请问有中文版的旅游手册吗?	Excuse me, is there a Chinese travel guide?
旅游手册在那里,请自行取用。	Travel guides are over there. Please be free to get.
我想询问旅游一日券的事情。	I'd like to ask about the one-day tour voucher.
我需要走路还是坐地铁呢?	Do I need to walk or take the subway?

♪ 060

用一日券能免费参观这些景点吗？	Is it free to visit these sights with the one-day tour voucher?
是的，费用包含这些景点的门票。	Yes, the fee includes the admissions of these sights.
你有推荐的其他景点吗？	Do you recommend other sights?
这个地方离这里很远吗？	Is this place far away from here?
走路约 10 分钟。	It's about a ten-minute walk.
你能在地图上为我讲解目的地吗？	Could you explain the destination on the map for me?
景点附近有什么地标吗？	**Are there any landmarks near the sights?**

博物馆

开放时间是几点到几点呢？	When does it open?
早上 7 点到下午 4 点。	It starts from 7 o'clock in the morning to 4 o'clock in the afternoon.
有租借语音导览的服务吗？	Is there the service for an audio guide?

走吧！一起用英语去旅行！

公休日是什么时候？	When is the official holiday?
周四公休。	We are closed on Thursdays.
每天都开放参观。	It's open for visits every day.
入口在哪里呢？	**Where is the entrance?**
请问售票亭在哪里呢？	Excuse me, where is the ticket booth?
请问门票多少钱？	Excuse me, how much is for the admission?
大人60美元，小孩45美元。	USD 60 for an adult, and USD 45 for a child.
我要两张全票，谢谢。	**I'd like two full-fare tickets, please.**
今天开放参观到几点？	**What time is open for visiting today?**
最近有什么特别的展览吗？	Is there any special exhibition recently?
有中文版的导览手册吗？	Is there any Chinese guide brochure?

哪里可以看到《蒙娜丽莎的微笑》呢？	Where can I see the picture of *the Mona Lisa*?
博物馆的常设展示在这个展览厅里吗？	Are the permanent displays of the museum in this exhibition hall?
博物馆里面可以喝水吗？	Can I drink water in the museum?
不好意思，馆内禁止饮食。	Sorry, it's forbidden to drink and eat in the museum.
我可以拍照吗？	May I take a picture?
馆内禁止摄影或录影。	It's prohibited to shoot or record in the museum.
博物馆里有置物柜吗？	Is there any locker in the museum?

展览馆

参观方向是往这里走吗？	Is the way for the visit?
这个展览是往这个方向走吗？	**Is the direction to this display?**
请问在哪里可以拿到展览简介？	Excuse me, where can I get some brief introduction of the exhibition?

♪ 063

专人导览是几点开始呢？	When does it start for the specialist guides?
请问你们有专人导览吗？	Excuse me, do you have any specialist guides?
↓ 专人导览服务需要事先申请。	It needs to apply for the service of specialist guides beforehand.
可以租借中文的语音导览机吗？	Can I rent a Chinese audio tour device?
↓ 好的，租借费为一次50美元。	No problem, it'll be USD 50 each time.
暂时离开展馆后可以再次入场吗？	Can I get into the exhibition once again after leaving for a while?
请问纪念品贩卖店在哪里？	Excuse me, where is the souvenir shop?

艺廊

请问参观需要门票或邀请函吗？	Excuse me, are admission tickets or invitation cards required if visiting?
↓ 不用，欢迎自由参观。	No, it's free to visit.

现在展览的是哪位艺术家的画作呢？	Which artist's paintings are being displayed now?
有这张画作的复印品可以购买吗？	Is there any copy product of this painting to buy?

教堂

大家是来这座大教堂祈求什么？	What does everybody pray for coming to this cathedral?
可以告诉我参观大教堂的方法吗？	Could you tell me what the way is to make a formal visit in the cathedral?
我想要为家人祈求身体健康。	I'd like to pray for my family's health.
这座大教堂有多少年的历史？	How many years are for the history of this cathedral?
请问这个徽章多少钱？	Excuse me, how much is this badge?
刚好有人在教堂举办婚礼。	Someone happened to hold the wedding in the church.
不知道是否可以参观弥撒仪式。	I wonder whether we can visit Mass or not.

♪ 065

我想要去_____。

I want to go to (the) _____.

[芝加哥]

Michigan Mile
密歇根大道

Chicago Botanic Garden
芝加哥植物园

Shedd Aquarium
谢德水族馆

Navy Pier
海军码头

Willis Tower
威利斯大厦

Tribune Tower
['trɪbjuːn 'taʊə]
论坛报大厦

Millennium Park
千禧公园

Art Institute of Chicago
芝加哥艺术博物馆

Adler Planetarium
阿德勒天文馆

[纽约]

Grant Park
格兰特公园

Museum of Natural History
纽约自然历史博物馆

Metropolitan Museum of Art
纽约大都会博物馆

Statue of Liberty
自由女神像

Yankee Stadium
洋基球场

Brooklyn Bridge
布鲁克林桥

Central Park	**Times Square**	**Empire State Building**	**5th Avenue**
['sentrəl pɑːk]	[taɪmz skweə]	['empaɪə steɪt 'bɪldɪŋ]	[fɪfθ 'ævənjuː]
中央公园	时代广场	帝国大厦	第五大道

Wall Street	**Broadway Show**		**Grand Canyon**
['wɔːl striːt]	['brɔːdweɪ ʃəʊ]		[grænd 'kænjən]
华尔街	百老汇	[其他景点]	大峡谷

Miami Beach	**Honolulu**	**Yellowstone National Park**	**Niagara Falls**
[maɪ'æmi biːtʃ]	[ˌhɒnə'luːluː]	['jeləuˌstəun'næʃnəl pɑːk]	[naɪ'ægərə fɔːlz]
迈阿密海滩	火奴鲁鲁	黄石公园	尼亚加拉大瀑布

Queen Ann	**Waterfront**	**NASA**	**Disneyland**
[kwiːn æn]	['wɔːtəfrʌnt]	['næsə]	['dɪznilænd]
安皇后区	海岸码头区	美国国家航天局	迪士尼乐园

Skywalk
['skaɪwɔːk]
天空步道

出发前 | 机场相关 | 国外住宿 | 观光景点 | 异国美食 | 购物乐趣 | 国外交通 | 紧急状况

单词

[迪士尼乐园]

roller coaster
[ˈrəʊlə kəʊstə]
过山车

merry-go-round
[ˈmeri gəʊ raʊnd]
旋转木马

monorail
[ˈmɒnəʊreɪl]
游园小火车

animation
[ˌænɪˈmeɪʃn]
动画

floating parade
[ˈfləʊtɪŋ pəˈreɪd]
花车游行

[其他景点]

art museum
[ɑːt mjuːˈzɪəm]
美术馆

park
[pɑːk]
公园

free fall
[friː fɔːl]
自由落体

museum
[mjuːˈziːəm]
博物馆

zoo
[zuː]
动物园

aquarium
[əˈkweərɪəm]
水族馆

canal
[kəˈnæl]
运河

beach
[biːtʃ]
海岸

night scene
[naɪt siːn]
夜景

deck
[dek]
展望台

shopping street
[ˈʃɒpɪŋ striːt]
商店街

Chinatown
[ˈtʃaɪnətaʊn]
唐人街

shopping mall
[ˈʃɒpɪŋ mɔːl]
购物中心

outlet
[ˈaʊtlet]
折扣店

♪ 068

entertaining rides [,entə'teɪrɪŋ raɪdz] 游乐设施	[旅游资讯中心]		**subway map** ['sʌbweɪ mæp] 地铁图
mascot ['mæskət] 吉祥物	**advertising DM** ['ædvətaɪzɪŋ ,di: 'em] 宣传 DM	**map** [mæp] 地图	
traveling pamphlet ['trævlɪŋ 'pæmflət] 旅游手册	**ticket** ['tɪkɪt] 交通券（票卡）	**admission** [əd'mɪʃn] 参观门票	**staff** [stɑ:f] 服务人员
line up [laɪn ʌp] 排队	**queue** [kju:] 排队人龙	**line route** [laɪn ru:t] 排队路线	**butt in line** [bʌt ɪn laɪn] 插队
[景点内部]	**visit entrance** ['vɪzɪt 'entrəns] 参观出入口	**elevator** ['elɪveɪtə] 电梯	**stairs** [steəz] 楼梯
information desk [,ɪnfə'meɪʃn desk] 服务台	**restroom** ['restru:m] 洗手间		
shopping department ['ʃɒpɪŋ dɪ'pɑ:tmənt] 商品部	**postcard** ['pəustkɑ:d] 明信片	**ticket booth** ['tɪkɪt bu:ð] 售票处	**souvenir badge** [,su:və'nɪə bædʒ] 纪念徽章
		**front desk** [frʌnt desk] 柜台	**souvenir** [,su:və'nɪə] 纪念品

美国大城市游览介绍

走吧！一起自由地探索大城市的各个角落

纽约

中央公园（Central Park）

位于曼哈顿中心，于1857年开放，其景观经过精心设计，有人工湖、滑冰场、野生动物保护区、游乐场，漫长的步行路径吸引了慢跑者、自行车骑行者前来。

公园的东边是第五大道、西边是中央公园西街、南边是哥伦布圆环与中央公园南街、北边是中央公园北街。

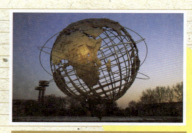

法拉盛草地公园（Flushing Meadows–Corona Park）

纽约的第二大公园，里面有美术馆、科学馆、剧院、人工湖、球场等。1964年的世界博览会在此举办，当时为了向世界宣告美国已进入太空新纪元而设立的140英尺[①]高的地球仪，至今仍是著名的景点。

迈阿密

阳光、沙滩、美女，塑造了迈阿密的迷人风景。

① 1英尺=0.3048米。

波特兰

波特兰因为气候适合种玫瑰，又被称为"玫瑰之城"，其区域内公园很多，甚至有座死火山，吸引了许多自然爱好者。

新奥尔良

新奥尔良是艺术与美食之都，它有丰富的法式建筑，也是爵士乐的诞生地，其从二月中持续到三月初的 Mardi Gras 嘉年华，每年吸引了数百万人参加。

出发前 | 机场相关 | 国外住宿 | **观光景点** | 异国美食 | 购物乐趣 | 国外交通 | 紧急状况

徜徉在自然美景中！

花一天的时间，离开都市，拥抱大自然。

▎风景名胜

请问参观需要门票吗？	Excuse me, is it necessary for the ticket to visit?
这里是排队买门票的队伍吗？	Is this for the line to buy the admissions?
这里的风景真漂亮。	The scenery here is really beautiful.
好多旅游团哦！	There are many sightseeing groups!
可以麻烦你帮我拍张照吗？	Would you mind taking a picture of me?
好的，笑一个！	No problem, say "cheese"!
这座国家公园叫什么名字？	What's the name of this national park?
这里就是旅游书介绍的公园吗？	Is this the park introduced in the traveling book?
听说这里的瀑布很有名。	I've heard that the waterfalls here are very famous.
今天有机会观赏到日出吗？	Is there any chance to watch the sunrise today?

♪ 072

从这里可以看到自由女神吗？	Can we see the Statue of Liberty from here?
这棵神树几岁了？	What's the age of the divine tree?
请问厕所在哪里？	Could you tell me where the restroom is?
请问哪里可以抽烟呢？	Excuse me, where can I smoke?

赏枫

现在正是枫叶季。	It's the maple season right now.
你有推荐的赏枫地点吗？	Do you recommend any places for enjoying the autumn colors?
好多人会在枫树下野餐。	Many people have a picnic under the maple trees.
我们下星期将举办枫叶季活动。	We are going to throw the maple season activity next week.
橘红色的枫叶好漂亮。	Reddish orange maple leaves are so beautiful.
枫叶逐渐开始转红了。	Maple leaves are turning red gradually.

走吧！一起用英语去旅行！

这里是有名的赏枫景点吗？	**Is here the noted place to enjoy the autumn colors?**
好多人来这里观赏枫红。	There are many people coming here to enjoy the fall colors.
来赏枫的观光客好多。	There are many visitors appreciating maples.
人多到我无法好好拍照。	I couldn't take pictures well due to the crowd.
这附近有什么名胜古迹吗？	Are there any historical sites around here?
听说有搭船观赏枫叶的套装行程。	I've heard that there's a package of appreciating maples by ship.

赏雪

现在室外的气温几度呢？	**What's the temperature outside now?**
外面下雪了。	**It's snowing outside.**
刚好碰到降雪，我们真是幸运。	It happens to snow. How lucky we are!
还好室内有暖气。	Thanks to the heater inside.

我没有带手套，在哪里可以买呢？	I don't bring my gloves. Where can I buy them?
这里可以租借雪服吗？	Can I borrow snow clothes here?
有可以租滑雪器材的地方吗？	Are there any places to rent the skiing equipment?
我们可以在公园堆雪人吗？	Can we make a snowman in the park?
交通状况受到暴风雪的影响吗？	Is the traffic influenced by the snowstorm?
下雪会影响接下来的行程吗？	Does the snow affect the following schedule?

▎冲浪

这种天气真适合冲浪。	It's suitable to go surfing in this kind of weather.
我想尝试在大浪时冲浪。	I'd like to try to go surfing in the surge of the tide.
这里的海滩很有名。	It's known for its beach here.
真的吗？那我一定要尝试看看。	Really? Then I have to give it a try.

♪ 075

走吧！一起用英语去旅行！

| 酒店提供冲浪器具租借服务吗？ | Does the hotel provide the rent for the equipment of surfing? |

| 是的，您可以到柜台询问相关信息。 | Yes, you can ask for some related information from the reception counter. |

| 一定要住宿酒店才可以免费租借冲浪器具吗？ | Do I have to stay in the hotel so that I can rent the surfing equipment for free? |

| 不，租借两小时是免费的。 | 不好意思，投宿在本酒店的房客是免费的。 |

No, it's free to rent for two hours.　　Excuse me, it's free for the visitors in our hotel.

| 冲浪后还可以享用露天烧烤。 | After surfing, you also can enjoy the open-air barbecue. |

泛舟

| 要几个人才能够参加泛舟？ | How many people can go white rafting? |

| 基本上，需要八个人搭乘一艘船。 | Basically, eight people get in one boat. |

| 不会游泳的话，也能够泛舟吗？ | If one can't swim, can he or she go white rafting? |

| 参加者有年龄限制吗？ | **Is there any limitation for the age of participants?** |

♪ 076

一日旅行团

请问有半天的行程吗？	Excuse me, is there any schedule of the half-day tour?
有参观大峡谷的旅游团吗？	Is there any tour group to the Grand Canyon?
这个行程会去参观哪些地方？	Where are we going to visit during this tour?
集合地点在哪里？	Where is the assembling place?
↓ 在车站的1号出口集合。	We'll gather at the No.1 gate at the station.
旅行团几点出发？	What time does the tour group start off?
↓ 上午9点出发。	We're going to hit the road at nine in the morning.
这个旅行团总共有多少人呢？	How many people are there in the tour group?
请问导游会说中文吗？	Excuse me, does the tour guide speak Chinese?
我们可以中途加入这个团吗？	Can we join in this group halfway?
旅行团会在什么时候结束呢？	When does the tour group end?

走吧！一起用英语去旅行！

费用包括接送或餐点吗？	Does the charge include picking up and dropping off or the meals?
不好意思，餐点需要自费。	Sorry, the meals are at your own expense.
可以让我们在喜来登酒店下车吗？	Can you drop us off at the Sheraton Hotel?
我想要报名参加这个旅行团。	**I'd like to register for this tour group.**
有其他推荐的行程吗？	**Do you recommend other tours?**

乘船观光

游览船的航程要多久呢？	How long will it take for go excursion boating?
一趟航程约 50 分钟。	It will take you around fifty minutes.
在游览船上，可以观赏沿岸的美景。	You can watch beautiful sceneries along the river on the excursion boat.
船上会有导游解说运河的历史。	The docent will explain the history of canals on the boat.

♪ 078

搭直升机

我想要搭直升机观赏纽约的夜景。	I'd like to take the helicopter to enjoy the night view of New York.
听说可以搭直升机游览大峡谷。	**I've heard that we can take the helicopter to travel the Great Canyon.**
不好意思,想请问收费方式?	Excuse me, could you tell me how to charge?
一趟 20 分钟,一个人大约 1500 美金。	It's around USD 1,500 for each person for 20 minutes.

纪念品专卖店

有推荐一定要买的纪念品吗?	**Do you recommend any must-buy souvenirs?**
这个图腾有什么特殊意义吗?	Does this totem have exceptional meanings?
国外旅客购买有优惠吗?	Is there any discount for foreign visitors to buy?
出示护照可以打九折哦。	You can get the 10 percent off if showing the passport.

♪ 079

句型

_____ 在哪里?
Where is the _____ ?

[交通地点]

train station
火车站

bus stop
公交车站

taxi stand
出租车停靠站

ticket vendor
自动售票机

platform
['plætfɔːm]
月台

add value machine
增值机

exit gate
[ˈeksɪt geɪt]
出口

parking lot
停车场

crosswalk
[ˈkrɒswɔːk]
人行横道

underground passage
地下通道

overpass
[ˈəʊvəpɑːs]
天桥

[金融机构]

automated teller machine
自动提款机

bank
[bæŋk]
银行

cash transfer machine
换钞机

ATM
自动提款机

coin machine
兑币机

bill
[bɪl]
钞票

change
[tʃeɪndʒ]
零钱

credit card
信用卡

credit card slip
刷卡单

[休闲地点]

restaurant
['restrɒnt]
餐厅

coffee shop
咖啡厅

pub
[pʌb]
酒吧

historical site
名胜古迹

night club
夜店

supermarket
['suːpəmaːkɪt]
超市

market
['maːkɪt]
市场

drugstore
['drʌgstɔː]
药妆店

shopping street
商业街

mall
[mɔːl]
购物中心

department store
百货公司

outlet
['aʊtlet]
品牌折扣店

bookstore
['bʊkstɔː]
书店

library
['laɪbrəri]
图书馆

bakery
['beɪkəri]
面包店

second-hand bookstore
二手书店

video rental store
影碟出租店

[个人物品]

cellphone
['selfəʊn]
手机

notebook
['nəʊtbʊk]
记事本

Wi-Fi shared device
Wi-Fi 分享器

passport
['paːspɔːt]
护照

mobile power pack
移动电源

出发前

机场相关

国外住宿

观光景点

异国美食

购物乐趣

国外交通

紧急状况

081

[一日游行程]

night scene
[naɪt siːn]
夜景

mountain climbing
登山

bungee jumping
蹦极

sightseeing
['saɪtsiːɪŋ]
观光

hiking
[haɪkɪŋ]
远足

paragliding
['pærəglaɪdɪŋ]
高空滑翔

hot-air-balloon
热气球

whale watching
赏鲸

snorkeling
['snɔːklɪŋ]
浮潜

scuba diving
深潜

surfing
['sɜːfɪŋ]
冲浪

white-rafting
泛舟

canoeing
[kə'nuːɪŋ]
划独木舟

skiing
['skiːɪŋ]
滑雪

[赏花]

spot of appreciating flowers
赏花地点

bloom season
[bluːm 'siːzn]
开花季

bud
[bʌd]
花苞

flower
['flaʊə]
花卉

bloomy
['bluːmɪ]
盛开的

petal
['petl]
花瓣

[赏枫]

place of appreciating maples
赏枫地点

yard
[jɑːd]
庭院

scenic spot
名胜

enjoy the autumn colors
赏枫

night view
[naɪt vjuː]
夜景

[海边]

beach
[biːtʃ]
沙滩

bathing beach
海水浴场

wave
[weɪv]
海浪

sea
[siː]
海

seashore
['siːʃɔː]
海滨

bikini
[bɪˈkiːni]
比基尼

swimsuit
['swɪmsuːt]
泳装

beach parasol
沙滩伞

beach chair
沙滩椅

swim trunks
泳裤

surfing board
冲浪板

kickboard
['kɪkbɔːd]
浮板

swimming ring
游泳圈

swimmer
['swɪmə]
游泳者

lifeguard
['laɪfgɑːd]
救生员

出发前 | 机场相关 | 国外住宿 | 观光景点 | 异国美食 | 购物乐趣 | 国外交通 | 紧急状况

♪ 083

美国的自然风光

除了热闹的市区，壮阔的自然风景也很吸引人！

大峡谷

大峡谷（Grand Canyon）位于亚利桑那州的西北部，于1979年被列入世界自然遗产，被誉为世界自然奇观之一。

大峡谷总长约446千米，最深处有1800米，是科罗拉多河经过数百万年的冲蚀，再加上板块的地理活动而形成。

最适合游览大峡谷的方式为徒步旅行、皮筏漂流，但因为大峡谷地形险峻，谷底的高温容易引起中暑，一般不建议做当天的往返，在徒步旅行时，也需要十分谨慎，避免受伤。

大峡谷于2007年3月启用"天空步道（skywalk）"，距离谷底约1200米，是世界上最高的空中走廊，为了安全起见，每次只准120人进入，入场费为25美元。

黄石公园

黄石公园（Yellowstone National Park）主要位于怀俄明州境内，部分位于蒙大拿、爱达荷州，是世界上第一个国家公园，它以丰富的野生动物、地热资源闻名。

著名的景点：老忠实喷泉、大棱镜彩泉、牵牛花温泉、黄石湖等。黄石公园也是许多大型动物的栖息地，包括美洲野牛、加拿大马鹿、灰熊、狼等，其境内的野牛群也是美国最古老的野牛群。

优胜美地国家公园

优胜美地国家公园（Yosemite National Park）位于加利福尼亚州，1984年被列入世界自然遗产。

壮观的花岗岩、清澈溪流与瀑布、巨杉等景致是优胜美地国家公园的特色。

尼亚加拉大瀑布

尼亚加拉大瀑布（Niagara Falls）景色美丽，它是位于五大湖区尼亚加拉河上的三座瀑布的总称，横跨美国纽约州与加拿大安大略省。

五大湖（Great Lakes）为：苏必利尔湖、休伦湖、密歇根湖、伊利湖、安大略湖。它们位于美国和加拿大交界处，除了密歇根湖全属美国之外，其他皆为两国共有。

夏威夷、阿拉斯加也很好玩

夏威夷

夏威夷（Hawaii）由夏威夷群岛组成，位于北太平洋中，距离美国本土3 700千米。因为夏威夷是由岛屿组成，因此空中交通很重要，其中又以檀香山国际机场（Honolulu International Airport）最重要。

夏威夷位于热带，经济主要是以旅游业为主，草裙舞、扶桑花、彩虹瀑布、冲浪、海岸、火山等，是一般人对于夏威夷的印象。美丽的热带风光吸引了世界各地的游客前往。除此之外，夏威夷也是许多新婚夫妻蜜月的首选地点。

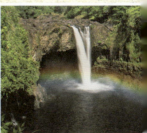

阿拉斯加

阿拉斯加（State of Alaska）是美国面积最大、最北边的州，阿拉斯加人常戏称美国本土为"lower 48"或者"Lower Forty-eight"。其旅游特色为：山脉、冰川、钓鱼、狩猎，也因为地理位置远离美国本土，许多人怀抱着自我放逐、寻找自我等心态选择前往阿拉斯加旅行。

Chapter 5 异国美食

民以食为天,出国就要勇于尝试当地的特色料理。不管是事先做好功课、查好餐厅,或是走到哪吃到哪、寻求当地人的建议,就让美味的食物为你的旅程增添更多风味吧!

去餐厅吃美食吧！

地方特色美食，没吃到就不算出国。

传统美食

欢迎光临。	Welcome.
我想要一份克里欧式料理。	**I'd like a Creole Style Cooking, please.**
一份卡真式料理。	Cajun Style Cooking, please.
我想要一份海鲜烩饭。	**I'm going to have Seafood Gumbo.**
我想要一份什锦炒饭。	I'm going to have Jambalaya, please.
你要小、中、大哪一种呢？	Cup, regular or large?
想要来点三寸超厚的比萨吗？	Would you like some Giordano's Pizza?
听起来很不错。	Sounds great.
小龙虾烩饭要加些辣椒调味料吗？	Would you like to add some cayenne pepper into Crawfish Etouffee?
小龙虾烩饭听起来很美味。	Crawfish Etouffee sounds delicious.

♪ 088

我可以再叫一份传统的夏威夷米饭吗？	May I have one more Loco Moco, please?
请问有两人的座位吗？	Is there a table for two?
请在此稍等，先填写这张点菜单。	Please wait here and fill in this order list.
我想加点巴西里香料。	I'd like some parsley, please.

海鲜自助餐

请问有订位吗？	Excuse me, do you have a reservation?
抱歉，没有。请问有12人的座位吗？	Sorry, we don't. Do you have a table for 12?
除了龙虾之外，还有牛排、鲑鱼等。	In addition to lobsters, there are steaks and salmon as well.
龙虾每人一次仅能拿一只。	Everyone just can get one lobster each time.
这生蚝吃起来真多汁。	This oyster tastes juicy.

走吧!一起用英语去旅行!

虾子配上芥末酱真是美味。	The shrimp tastes delicious with the mustard.
来碗海鲜清汤也不错。	It's good to have a bowl of seafood broth.
香煎干贝还要5分钟。	It takes five more minutes for scallops.
我可以多加一些酱料吗?	**May I add more seasoning?**
桌上的盐和黑胡椒可以自行取用。	The salt and black pepper on the table are free to take.

▌特殊需求

请不要加葱（蒜），谢谢。	Please do not add any green onion (garlic). Thank you.
请问有中文菜单吗?	**Do you have a menu in Chinese?**
浓汤是牛肉还是海鲜?	**Is the pottage beef or seafood?**
请问有素食餐点吗?	**Is there any vegetarian meal?**
请问有不含鱼或肉的蘸酱吗?	Is there any dressing without fish or meat?

下午茶

我想要奶酪蛋糕和一杯热水果茶。	**I'd like a cheese cake and a cup of hot fruit tea.**
我想要两个杯子蛋糕。	I'd like two cupcakes.
我想要一份烤薄饼，蜂蜜多一点。	I'd like a pancake with more honey.
推荐哪款蛋糕呢？	Is there any recommendation for cakes?
我推荐布朗尼，会附一球冰激凌。	I'll recommend brownies. It goes with a scoop of ice cream.
请问你们还有香蕉蛋糕吗？	Excuse me, do you still have banana cakes?
每日限定的草莓挞还有吗？	**Do you still have the daily strawberry tarts?**
这款蛋糕里含有坚果吗？	**Does this kind of cake have nuts inside?**
请问你们有咸的点心吗？	Do you have any salty snacks?
你可以试试我们的三明治。	You can try some sandwiches.

走吧！一起用英语去旅行！

| 请问下午茶的组合怎么算？ | How much is for the tea time set? |

| 不好意思，我想要点餐。 | Excuse me, I'm ready to order. |

咖啡店

| 请问你们有最低消费吗？ | Excuse me, do you have the minimum charge? |
| 每个人需点一杯饮料。 | Everyone needs to order a cup of drink. |

| 你们有推荐的单品咖啡吗？ | Do you recommend any single origin coffee? |
| 我们店的蓝山咖啡很不错。 | The Blue Mountain coffee tastes good in our shop. |

| 我想要一杯卡布奇诺，不加肉桂粉。 | **I'd like a cup of cappuccino without cinnamon.** |

| 我要一杯冰的美式咖啡，双倍浓缩。 | I'd like a cup of iced Americano with double espresso. |

| 一杯低咖啡因的香草拿铁，谢谢。 | One cup of low caffeine vanilla latte, please. |

我想要一杯热拿铁，不加糖。	I'd like a cup of hot latte without sugar.
请问你们是使用牛奶还是豆奶？	Excuse me, do you use milk or soymilk?
我习惯每天点一杯卡布奇诺。	I am used to order a cup of cappuccino every day.
你们用哪种咖啡豆？	What kind of coffee beans do you use?

[各种蛋糕甜点]

		chocolate cake 巧克力蛋糕
chiffon cake 戚风蛋糕	**Boston cream pie** 波士顿派	**mille-feuilles** 千层派
sponge cake 海绵蛋糕	**handmade cookie** 手工饼干	**custard tart** 蛋挞
cream caramel 焦糖布丁	**cream brulee** 烤布蕾	**passion fruit cheese** 百香果乳酪

句型

请给我_____。
May I have a / an _____?

[各地美食代表]

Jambalaya
[ˌdʒæmbəˈlaɪə]
什锦炒饭

Cajun Style Cooking
卡真式料理

Crawfish Etouffee
小龙虾烩饭

Giordano's Pizza
三寸超厚比萨

Creole Style Cooking
克里欧式料理

Seafood Gumbo
海鲜烩饭

Loco Moco
夏威夷式米饭

[海鲜]

lobster
[ˈlɒbstə]
大龙虾

salmon
[ˈsæmən]
鲑鱼

oyster
[ˈɔɪstə]
生蚝

shrimp
[ʃrɪmp]
虾子

scallop
[ˈskɒləp]
干贝

[酱料]

soy sauce
酱油

mustard
[ˈmʌstəd]
芥末

salt
[sɔːlt]
盐

vinegar
[ˈvɪnɪɡə]
醋

black pepper
黑胡椒粉

[配菜]

seafood broth
海鲜清汤

celery
['seləri]
芹菜

onion
['ʌnjən]
洋葱

pepper
['pepə]
甜椒

sausage
['sɒsɪdʒ]
香肠

croquette
[krəʊ'ket]
可乐饼

French fries
薯条

chicken nugget
炸鸡块

green onion
[griːn 'ʌnjən]
葱

garlic
['gɑːlɪk]
大蒜

[饮料]

hot tea
[hɒt tiː]
热茶

iced black (green) tea
冰红（绿）茶

coffee
['kɒfi]
咖啡

milk tea
[mɪlk tiː]
奶茶

juice
[dʒuːs]
果汁

iced water
[aɪst 'wɔːtə]
加冰块的水

出发前 | 机场相关 | 国外住宿 | 观光景点 | 异国美食 | 购物乐趣 | 国外交通 | 紧急状况

095

单词

[牛排]

A la cart
单点

Rib Eye Steak
肋眼牛排

T-bone Steak
丁骨牛排

set menu
套餐

main course
主餐

New York Steak
纽约厚牛排

Roasted Steak
炭烤牛排

Kobe Steak
神户牛排

bun
[bʌn]
餐包

appetizer
['æpɪtaɪzə]
开胃菜

side dish
附餐

medium-rare
三分熟

medium
['miːdrəm]
五分熟

medium-well
七分熟

well-done
[weɫ dʌn]
全熟

soup
[suːp]
汤

salad
['sæləd]
沙拉

[面类]

spaghetti
[spə'geti]
意大利细面

starter
['staːtə]
前菜

seafood chowder
海鲜浓汤

pasta
['pæstə]
意大利面

♪ 096

seafood pasta
海鲜意大利面

lasagna
[ləˈzænjə]
千层面

rotini
[ˈraʊtɪnɪ]
螺旋面

rigatoni
[ˌrɪgəˈtəʊnɪ]
通心粉

mushroom pasta
蘑菇意大利面

penne rigate
笔管面

[饭后甜点]

soufflé
[ˈsuːfleɪ]
法式舒芙蕾

clam pasta with white wine sauce
白酒蛤蜊意大利面

bavette
[baˈvet]
宽扁面

dessert
[dɪˈzɜːt]
甜点

mousse
[muːs]
慕斯

cream caramel
焦糖布丁

apple pie
苹果派

[附餐]

side dish
附餐

onion ring
洋葱圈

hash browns
薯饼

French fries
薯条

mashed potato
土豆泥

chicken nugget
鸡块

squid roll
鱿鱼卷

♪ 097

单词

[食材]

beef [biːf] 牛肉

pork [pɔːk] 猪肉

mutton ['mʌtn] 羊肉

meat [miːt] 肉类

chicken ['tʃɪkɪn] 鸡肉

egg [eg] 鸡蛋

fish [fɪʃ] 鱼肉

lobster ['lɒbstə] 龙虾

crab [kræb] 螃蟹

oyster ['ɔɪstə] 牡蛎

shellfish ['ʃelfɪʃ] 贝类

dough [dəʊ] 面团

noodles ['nuːdlz] 面条

mussel ['mʌsl] 淡菜

vegetable ['vedʒtəbl] 蔬菜

onion ['ʌnjən] 洋葱

carrot ['kærət] 胡萝卜

mushroom ['mʌʃrʊm] 香菇

cucumber ['kjuːkʌmbə] 黄瓜

corn [kɔːn] 玉米

potato [pə'teɪtəʊ] 马铃薯

♪ 098

[面包]

sandwich ['sænwɪtʃ] 三明治

croissant ['krwæsö] 可颂

bagel ['beɪgl] 百吉饼

toast [təʊst] 烤吐司

pancake ['pænkeɪk] 松饼

[饮料]

coffee ['kɒfi] 咖啡

Americano coffee 美式咖啡

beverage ['bevərɪdʒ] 饮料

latte ['lɑːteɪ] 拿铁

cappuccino [ˌkæpu'tʃiːnəʊ] 卡布其诺

green tea [griːn tiː] 绿茶

milk tea [mɪlk tiː] 奶茶

espresso [e'spresəʊ] 意式浓缩咖啡

mocha ['mɒkə] 摩卡

black tea [blæk tiː] 红茶

fruit tea [fruːt tiː] 水果茶

juice [dʒuːs] 果汁

hot chocolate [hɒt 'tʃɒklət] 热巧克力

soda pop ['səʊdə pɒp] 汽水

Coke [kəʊk] 可乐

出发前 | 机场相关 | 国外住宿 | 观光景点 | **异国美食** | 购物乐趣 | 紧急状况 | 旅游情报

不可不知的餐桌礼仪

各国的餐桌礼仪各有不同，小心别在餐厅失礼了！

餐具摆设

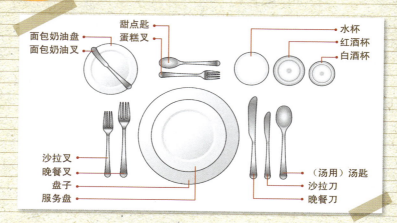

- 面包奶油盘
- 面包奶油叉
- 甜点匙
- 蛋糕叉
- 水杯
- 红酒杯
- 白酒杯
- 沙拉叉
- 晚餐叉
- 盘子
- 服务盘
- （汤用）汤匙
- 沙拉刀
- 晚餐刀

各式杯子

　　从座位的分配可以看出关系的亲疏，一般面向正门者为上座，坐主人右手边的客人为主客。而在座位的安排上，通常是男士女士、熟人生人交叉排列，就算是夫妇也会以对角方式错开而坐，主要是为了通过座位的安排，让宾客互相认识，用餐气氛也更加热闹。

　　一般入座时会由椅子的左侧就座，若是在餐厅用餐，须由服务人员带位，切勿自行入座。而在用餐期间，避免中途离开处理事务，吃东西时则应避免发出声音或是打嗝、打喷嚏，女士更要特别留意，不要在杯子边缘留下口红印，若需要补妆，应前往化妆室，避免在大家面前补妆。

　　杯子通常会放在餐具的右上角，依据杯子的款式不同，其盛装的饮料也不大一样，通常基本会有水杯、红葡萄酒的杯子、白葡萄酒的杯子。而盛装所点的饮料（例如：香槟等），会再提供适用的杯子。

装水用的高脚杯　　装红葡萄酒用的高脚杯　　装白葡萄酒用的高脚杯

刀叉使用方式

餐具的取用是由外而内，在使用时，一般为右手拿刀、左手拿叉，叉子除了可以压住食物、叉食东西之外，也可以舀食豆类或米饭。刀叉用得优雅，也就能吃得优雅。

喝汤、吃面包的礼仪

汤品

1. 喝汤盘里的汤，需用大汤匙由内而外舀食；喝有双耳汤杯里的汤，用附带的小汤匙试过温度后，可直接端至口边饮用。
2. 喝汤时，不可发出声音，也不可吹气将汤吹凉。喝完之后，汤匙应放在底盘或盘中，汤柄在右边，汤匙的凹陷处向上。

面包

1. 食用时，应左手拿面包，右手将面包撕成小块，再以左手拿面包，右手涂抹奶油。
2. 需使用奶油刀涂抹奶油，若奶油刀为共用的，要注意不可独占。

[刀叉摆设传递的意义]

刀叉摆设的方式，表达了你对于餐点的想法。

Start 开始用餐

Excellent 绝佳

Don't like 不喜欢

Pause
暂停一下，还要继续用餐

Ready for next plate
准备好吃下一道

Finished 食用完毕

超级市场也有好吃的！

国外的超级市场东西超丰富，一定要去逛。

超级市场

我可以到超级市场里购买三餐食材。	I can buy foods for meals in the supermarket.
沙拉没有了，你们什么时候会补货呢？	It's out of salad. When will you replenish the stock?
热食和饮料请帮我分开放。	Please help me put the hot food and drinks into different bags.
不用袋子，谢谢。	No bags, thank you.
请问需要叉子吗？	Do you need forks?
是的，也请给我汤匙。	Yes, and spoons, please.
我可以用信用卡结账吗？	May I pay by / with credit card?
可以，请将卡片放在这里。	Sure. Please put your credit card here.
收你现金 100 元。	Take your cash 100 dollars.

鲜食类

这里卖三明治吗？	Can I buy some sandwiches here?
超级市场还卖烤鸡呢！	The supermarket also sells roasted chicken!
我想买盒可颂当早餐吃。	I'm going to buy a box of croissants for breakfast.
买甜点去公园吃听起来不错。	It sounds good to buy some desserts to have in the park.
食物上的标签写了保质期限。	The expiration date is marked on the label of food.
面包里的是猪肉还是金枪鱼？	Is it for pork or tuna inside?
沙拉的选择好多哦！	There are many choices for salads!
我想试试看超级市场里的烤鸡。	I'd like to try the roasted chicken in the supermarket.
这个马铃薯沙拉看起来好好吃。	The potato salad looks pretty yummy.
我爱吃超级市场里的蛋挞。	I love the egg tarts from the supermarket.

走吧！一起用英语去旅行！

微波食品

请问小圆面包需要微波吗？	Do these buns need to be microwaved?
你可以不加热就直接食用。	You can have them without being heated.
这些熟水饺要微波多久？	How long will I microwave for these cooked dumplings?
这个三明治不微波也可以吃吗？	Can I have this sandwich without being microwaved?

饼干糖果类

我朋友推荐我买这款巧克力。	My friend recommends me to buy this kind of chocolate.
这款饼干好好吃。	This type of cookie tastes good.
每间店都有各自的限量商品。	There are limited goods in every shop.
小包的糖果很适合当伴手礼。	Small-packaged candy is suitable for souvenirs.

面包甜点类

这间店提供现烤面包。	The shop supplies fresh baked bread.
冰柜里的蛋糕看起来真美味。	The cakes in the freezer look so yummy.
芦荟酸奶好还是草莓酸奶好？	Is the aloe yogurt good or the strawberry one?
我想顺便买个甜点当点心。	I'd like to buy some desserts for snacks conveniently.
这款蛋糕很好吃。	This kind of cake is very delicious.
如果我买一些法国面包的话，你们可以帮我切成小块吗？	If I buy some French bread, will you cut it into pieces for me?
不好意思，我们不提供这样的服务。	Sorry, we don't have this kind of service.

饮料类

在美国很难买到难喝的咖啡。	In America, it's hard to buy unpleasant coffee.
我想喝杯现煮意式浓缩咖啡。	I'd like to have a cup of fresh made Espresso.

走吧！一起用英语去旅行！

有没有来美国一定要喝的饮料？	Are there any beverages needed to drink when coming to America?
这两瓶饮料正在促销吗？	**Are these two bottles of drinks on sale?**
请问有不冰的水吗？	**Excuse me, is there any water without ice?**
对我来说，美国的巧克力奶茶太甜了。	For me, American chocolate milk tea is too sweet.
果蔬汁的选择好多。	There are many choices for fruit and vegetable juice.
一定要喝喝看这款芒果冰沙。	You have to drink this kind of mango smoothie.
可乐竟然卖得比水还要便宜。	Coke is even much cheaper than water.

购买须知

在这间超市购物，需要办会员卡吗？	**Do we need to apply for a member card in this supermarket?**
这里的商品分量都好大。	It has a large quantity of every item here.

请问超市提供塑料袋吗？	Excuse me, do you offer plastic bags in the supermarket?
我们只提供纸袋。	We only offer paper bags.
这里的东西可以免费试吃。	The food here is free to take a bite.
这种薯片口味只有在美国才能买到。	This flavor of potato chips just can be bought in America.
因为圣诞假期，很多人来超市采买。	Because of the Christmas holiday, many people go shopping in the supermarket.
超市的手推车可以推到停车场再归还。	The shopping cart of the supermarket can be returned when pushing to the parking lot.
请问可以刷卡结账吗？	Excuse me, can I pay by / with credit card?
不好意思，这里是现金专用结账柜台。	I'm sorry. This is the counter for cash.

♪ 107

句型

_____多少钱?

How much is the _____?

[生鲜食物]

fried chicken 炸鸡	**mashed potato** 土豆泥	**sandwich** ['sænwɪtʃ] 三明治	**corn chowder** 玉米浓汤
French fries [frentʃ fraɪz] 薯条			
salad ['sæləd] 沙拉	[微波食品]	**hamburger** ['hæmbɜːgə] 汉堡	**Shaw Mai** 烧卖
cooked dumpling 熟水饺			**tomato cheese pizza** 番茄乳酪比萨
bun [bʌn] 小圆面包	**cream corn croquette** 奶油玉米可乐饼	**risotto** [rɪ'zɒtəʊ] 炖饭	**cooked rice** 熟饭
[饼干糖果]	**potato chips** 薯片	**rice cracker** 米果	**chocolate bar** 巧克力棒
	pretzel ['pretsl] 椒盐脆饼	**sea weed** 海苔	**oreo** ['ɔːrian] 奥利奥饼干

soya bean 毛豆

marshmallow [,mɑːʃˈmæləʊ] 棉花糖	**macadamia nuts** 夏威夷豆	**jelly bean** 雷根糖	**gummy bear** 小熊软糖
dried shredded squid 鱿鱼丝	**fascini scoox** 水果糖	**beef jerky** 牛肉条	**lollipop** [ˈlɒlɪpɒp] 棒棒糖

[甜点饮料]

cake [keɪk] 蛋糕	**cream caramel** 焦糖布丁	**panna cotta** 意式奶酪

canned beverage 罐装饮料	**bottled beverage** 瓶装饮料	**foil packaged beverage** 铝箔包饮料	**family sized beverage** 家庭装饮料

请给我_____。

Please give me (a / an)_____.

		knife [naɪf] 刀	**fork** [fɔːk] 叉
spoon [spuːn] 汤匙	**coffee spoon** 咖啡匙	**stirring bar** 搅拌棒	**straw** [strɔː] 吸管

单词

[食物区]

cookie ['kʊki] 饼干

candy ['kændi] 糖果

dessert [dɪˈzɜːt] 甜点

food [fuːd] 食物

instant noodles ['ɪnstənt 'nuːdlz] 泡面

boxed meal 盒装快餐

vegetable ['vedʒtəbl] 青菜

ice cream 冰激凌

dressing ['dresɪŋ] 酱料

popsicle ['pɒpsɪkl] 冰棒

expiration date 保质期限

[饮料区]

black tea 红茶

matcha ['mætʃə] 抹茶

marked price 标价

drinks [drɪŋks] 饮料

green tea 绿茶

milk tea 奶茶

matcha latte 抹茶拿铁

milk [mɪlk] 牛奶

beer [bɪə] 啤酒

fruit wine 水果酒

fruit and vegetable juice 果蔬汁

[报纸杂志区]

newspaper
['njuːzpeɪpə]
报纸

magazine
[ˌmægə'ziːn]
杂志

tabloid magazine
['tæblɔɪd ˌmægə'ziːn]
八卦杂志

flyer
['flaɪə]
广告单

paperback
['peɪpəbæk]
平装本

comic book
漫画书

video game CD
游戏光碟

[杂物区]

digital video disk
影音光碟（DVD）

disposable underwear
免洗内衣裤

battery
['bætri]
电池

adapter
[ə'dæptə]
转接头

tissue
['tɪʃuː]
面纸

tampon
['tæmpɒn]
卫生棉

mask
[mɑːsk]
口罩

[柜台区]

cash register
收银机

invoice
['ɪnvɔɪs]
发票

clerk
[klɑːk]
店员

barcode printer
条码机

cigarette
[ˌsɪgə'ret]
香烟

♪ 111

不可不知的牛肉

牛排是餐厅的常见菜色，但每个部位的口感与价位都不一样！

牛肉介绍

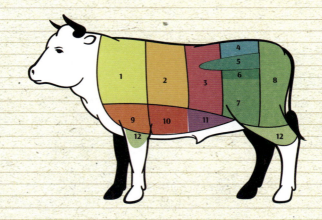

1. chuck 牛肩胛肉
2. rib 肋骨肉（肋眼牛排、牛小排）
3. short loin 里脊肉（纽约客牛排、丁骨牛排）
4. sirloin 里脊肉（沙朗牛排）
5. tenderloin 腰内肉（菲力牛排）
6. top sirloin 靠背部的里脊肉
7. bottom sirloin 靠腹部的里脊肉
8. round 臀肉、后腿肉（牛腱）
9. brisket 胸肉
10. plate 腹肉
11. flank 腹肉
12. shank 腿肉（牛腱）

非吃不可的牛排

牛排是西式餐点中最常见的主菜,它是块状的牛肉,一般以煎或烤的方式烹调。而依照牛肉部位的不同,牛排种类也不同,例如:

1. 肋骨肉部位的牛排有肋眼牛排、牛小排。
2. 里脊肉部位的牛排有纽约客牛排、丁骨牛排、沙朗牛排。
3. 腰内肉部位的牛排有菲力牛排。
4. 腹肉可以做牛小排。
5. 臀肉、后腿肉则有牛腱。

丁骨牛排

取自于牛的前腰脊部位,由纽约客牛排与一小部分的菲力牛排组合而成,丁骨牛排中间的丁骨,便是分界线。以口感来说,菲力牛排较为鲜嫩,而纽约客牛排则有嚼劲,菲力牛排精瘦,纽约客牛排则较多油花,一份丁骨牛排可同时吃到两种口感,建议熟度为三到五分熟。

牛排熟度

一般牛排不大会烹至全熟,外国人喜欢吃三分熟或五分熟,三分熟的牛排会呈现外围灰褐色,剖面为血红色,五分熟的牛排剖面则为粉红色,但核心仍保有血红色。但也有一部分人则是习惯吃七分熟,七分熟的牛排剖面则全为粉红色,若对于吃带红色的肉有恐惧感的话,也可以吃全熟。

全生 (raw)

一分熟 (rare)

三分熟 (medium rare)

五分熟 (medium)

七分熟 (medium well)

全熟 (well done)

每种牛排都有适合食用的熟度,例如肋眼牛排一般推荐吃五到七分熟,菲力牛排因为过熟的话,肉质会变硬,无法品尝到鲜嫩多汁的口感,所以建议熟度为三分熟,纽约客牛排和丁骨牛排都是建议三分到五分熟即可。

不可不知的猪肉

除了牛肉之外,最常见的肉类食物便是猪肉了!

猪肉介绍

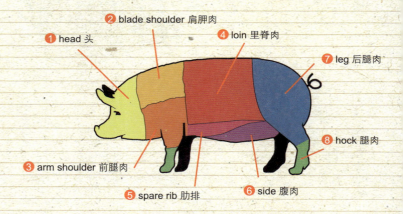

1. head 头
2. blade shoulder 肩胛肉
3. arm shoulder 前腿肉
4. loin 里脊肉
5. spare rib 肋排
6. side 腹肉
7. leg 后腿肉
8. hock 腿肉

猪肉料理

碳烤肋排

不管是餐厅,还是自家烤肉,碳烤肋排都是很受欢迎的食物。肋排先腌制或是烟熏之后,整片放到炭火上烧烤,烤至表皮有点焦,并有烧烤的痕迹即可,碳烤的香味让肋排变得更好吃。

德国猪脚

另一个常见的猪肉料理是"德国猪脚",猪脚会先腌制并煮过后,再用烤箱烤到表皮酥脆即可,通常会很豪迈地将整只猪脚装盘上桌,食用时,一般会搭配薯条或薯块、德国酸菜、芥末酱等。

其他常见肉类料理

羊排

羊排料理其实很简单，只要稍微抹上盐巴，用平底锅或是烤箱烤即可，重点在于肉的表面必须上色。上桌时，可以运用羊排的形状与骨头位置，做出不同感觉的摆盘。

鸡肉

鸡肉是最常食用的禽肉，一般会做成烤鸡或是炸鸡。利用全鸡或是部分鸡肉做的烤鸡，通常会先腌制再烤，烤的过程中，会涂抹酱汁，使其更加入味。炸鸡，顾名思义是用油炸做的鸡肉料理，通常会使用部分鸡肉，油炸的方式和油炸时裹的粉，这些元素形成了各种不同口感的炸鸡。

烤火鸡

若刚好碰到感恩节，那一定会吃烤火鸡。通常火鸡需要腌制两到三天，火鸡里面会塞满香料，再进烤箱烘烤两到三个小时，烤至表皮金黄即可，食用时，可搭配酱料或肉汁一起食用。

[各种调味料]

saffron ['sæfrən] 番红花	**garlic** ['gɑːlɪk] 大蒜
rosemary ['rəuzməri] 迷迭香	**thyme** [taɪm] 百里香
basil ['bæzl] 罗勒	**paprika** [pə'priːkə] 辣椒粉

去小酒馆干一杯！

啤酒、好友，多么惬意的一晚。

小酒馆

我们去小酒馆喝一杯吧。	Let's drink in the tavern.
我的主餐要烤鸡胸肉。	I'd like a roasted chick breast for the entrée.
好的，请问还需要点什么吗？	Sure, what else?
你们有主厨推荐餐点吗？	**Do you have the chef's recommendation?**
再来一杯长岛冰茶。	**One more Long Island Iced Tea, please.**
我们可以一起分享安格斯汉堡。	We can share the Angus Burger with each other.
淡菜配上一点啤酒也不错。	Mussels with a bit of beer is a good idea.
想要来些烤鸡翅吗？	Would you like some roasted chicken wings?
大部分的人都点什么吃呢？	What do most people order?
请问鸡翅有辣味的吗？	**Do you have spicy chicken wings?**

听说这里的肋排非常好吃。	I've heard that ribs here are very delicious.
可以先上开胃菜吗？	May I have the appetizer first?

比萨店

你好，请问需要点餐吗？	Hi, are you ready to order?
我想要点一份海鲜比萨，谢谢。	I'd like to order a seafood pizza, please.
不好意思，这里需要加点。	Excuse me, we are going to take an extra order.
好的，稍等一下，马上为你服务。	Alright, please wait a moment. I'll serve you at once.
主厨沙拉可以先上。	Chef's salad can be served first.
夏威夷比萨一份，谢谢。	A Hawaiian, please.
饼皮是要厚的还是薄的呢？	Would you prefer the pastry thick or thin?
这家店的食材都是产地直送的。	The ingredients are directly delivered from the places of origin at this restaurant.

这家店的食物真是名不虚传。	The food of this restaurant well deserves its reputation.

▌酒水类

我想要三杯啤酒。	I'd like three glasses of beer.
请问要罐装的还是瓶装的呢?	Would you like canned or bottled beer?
烈酒一杯。	A shot, please.
不好意思,请再给我一杯血腥玛丽。	Excuse me, I'd like another glass of Bloody Mary.
这些啤酒是你能喝的极限了吗?	Is the beer for all you can drink?
请给我一个冰桶,谢谢。	**Please give me an ice bucket. Thank you.**
不含酒精的饮料有哪些?	**What are there for soft drinks?**
我想要喝些鸡尾酒。	I'd like to have some cocktails.

早餐店

我想要小圆面包配培根。	I'd like some buns with bacon.
香肠配上煎蛋卷也是一种不错的选择。	It's also a good taste to have the sausage with omelet.
你要喝杯咖啡或是牛奶吗？	**Would you like some coffee or milk?**
我想要两个荷包蛋和三片火腿肉。	**I'm going to have two sunny-side-up eggs and three pieces of ham.**
这里的火腿有好多选择。	There are many choices of ham here.
水煮蛋加些胡椒粉尝起来真美味。	It tastes delicious to add some black pepper onto the boiled egg.
你可以尝试在烤吐司里夹上花生酱和蓝莓果酱。	You can try a piece of toast with peanut butter and blueberry jam.
这奶精配红茶或配咖啡都好喝。	It tastes good to add this coffee mate into black tea or coffee.

走吧！一起用英语去旅行！

牛排馆

我想要一份沙朗牛排。	I'd like a sirloin steak.
请问要几分熟呢？	How would you like your steak?
五分熟，谢谢。	Medium, please.
有推荐的套餐吗？	**Is there any recommendation for the combination?**
请问餐点有附汤吗？	Does this meal go with soup?
不好意思，汤要另外点。	Sorry, you need to order an extra soup.
沙拉的选择有哪些呢？	**What are choices of salad?**
我想点一份海陆大餐。	I'd like to order a Surf and Turf Combo.

座位

请问有可容纳30人的包厢吗？	Is there a stateroom for thirty people?
现场候位的话，需要等多久呢？	How long is the wait?

请问有四个人的位子吗？
Is there a table for four?

有的，里面请。
Yes, please follow me.

不好意思，现在客人很多。
Sorry, it's crowded with customers.

结账

你好，我想要结账。
Hi, I'd like to check out.

请问是到前台结账吗？
Excuse me, should I pay at the front desk?

不好意思，我没有点这个。
Sorry, I didn't order this.

总共是多少钱？
How much is the total cost?

您的账单总共是 300 美元。
Your bill comes to three hundred U.S. dollars.

今天的消费金额为 250 美元，收您信用卡。
The total today is USD 250. Take your credit card.

麻烦请您在签单上签名。
Please kindly put down your signature here on this receipt.

走吧！一起用英语去旅行！

请问您要刷卡还是付现？	Would you like to pay by / with credit card or in cash?
刷卡，谢谢。	Credit card, please.
我要付现，谢谢。	I'm going to pay in cash, please.
请问可以给我收据吗？	Could you give me a receipt, please?
这里是 200 美元，零钱不用找了。	Here is USD 200, and keep the change.
请帮我刷卡，再加 10 元当小费。	I'd like to pay by / with credit card, including 10 dollars for a tip.
账单上的总金额是正确的吗？	Is the total on the bill correct?

表达不满

不好意思，我点的餐点还没有送来。	Excuse me, my order hasn't been served.
我的餐点来了，但我女朋友的餐点还没来。	My order is here, but my girlfriend's hasn't been served.
我们的餐点还没来，麻烦你确认一下。	Our meals haven't been served. Please confirm them for us.

不好意思，这道烤鸡胸肉还有点生。	Excuse me, the roasted chicken breast is a little bit raw.
我点的是五分熟，但这块肉是七分熟。	The steak I ordered is medium, but it is medium-well.
我点的是牛肉，但你送来的是鸡肉。	I ordered beef, but you served chicken.
消费明细上的啤酒我没有点。	There's beer what I didn't order on the bills.
这个杯子是脏的，可以换新的吗？	**This glass is dirty. May I have a new one?**

表达赞扬

谢谢你贴心的服务。	Thanks for your nice service.
谢谢你推荐这道菜，很好吃。	Thank you for recommending this dish. It's really tasty.
今天的餐点很好吃，帮我向主厨致谢。	**Today's meal is very delicious. Please say thanks to the Chef for me.**
你推荐的红酒和餐点很搭。	The red wine you recommend goes well with this meal.

句型

请给我_____。
Please give me _____.

[食物]

butternut squash
白胡桃泥

chicken nugget
炸鸡块

fried shrimp
炸虾

mussel
['mʌsl]
淡菜

sirloin
['sɜ:lɔɪn]
沙朗牛排

fried oyster
炸牡蛎

roasted pork
烤猪肉

roasted chicken
[rəustɪd 'tʃɪkɪn]
烤鸡肉

roasted chicken wing
烤鸡翅

Caesar salad
[,si:zə 'sæləd]
恺撒沙拉

Surf & Turf Combo
海陆大餐

Garden salad
田园沙拉

[酒类饮料]

beer
[bɪə]
啤酒

Bloody Mary
血腥玛丽

Long Island Iced Tea
长岛冰茶

cocktail
['kɒkteɪl]
鸡尾酒

soft drinks
不含酒精饮料

ice cube bucket
冰桶

shot
[ʃɒt]
烈酒

[食材]

vegetable
['vedʒtəbl]
青菜

onion
['ʌnjən]
洋葱

bean sprouts
豆芽菜

turnip
['tɜːnɪp]
白萝卜

carrot
['kærət]
胡萝卜

mushroom
['mʌʃrum]
蘑菇

loofah
['luːfə]
丝瓜

Jew's-ear
['dʒuːzɪə]
黑木耳

broccoli
['brɒkəli]
西兰花

Chinese cabbage
白菜

cabbage
['kæbɪdʒ]
卷心菜

seafood
['siːfuːd]
海鲜

sausage
['sɒsɪdʒ]
香肠

boiled egg
[ˌbɔɪld eg]
水煮蛋

sunny-side-up egg
荷包蛋

scrambled egg
炒蛋

bacon
['beɪkən]
培根

出发前 | 机场相关 | 国外住宿 | 观光景点 | 异国美食 | 购物乐趣 | 国外交通 | 紧急状况

[调味料]

soy sauce 酱油

vinegar ['vɪnɪgə] 醋

chili oil 辣油

flavoring ['fleɪvərɪŋ] 调味料

sesame oil 芝麻油

black pepper 黑胡椒粉

sea salt 海盐

[餐具]

plate [pleɪt] 盘子

shichimi 七味粉

rosemary 迷迭香

table cloth 桌布

chopsticks ['tʃɒpstɪks] 筷子

spoon [spuːn] 汤匙

napkin ['næpkɪn] 餐巾纸

toothpick ['tuːθpɪk] 牙签

opener ['əʊpnə] 开瓶器

dish [dɪʃ] 碟子

tray [treɪ] 餐盘

bowl [bəʊl] 碗

[菜单]

[菜单]	**seasonal menu** 季节菜单	**seasonal limited** 季节限定	**carefully selected** 严选
special menu 特色菜单	**seasonal food** 当季食材	**speciality** [ˌspeʃiˈæləti] 名产	**specialty** [ˈspeʃəlti] 特产
popularity [ˌpɒpjuˈlærəti] 人气	**buffet** [ˈbʊfeɪ] 自助餐	**[账单]**	**cash** [kæʃ] 现金
limited [ˈlɪmɪtɪd] 限定	**set meal** [set miːl] 套餐	**sum** [sʌm] 总金额	
credit card 信用卡	**item** [ˈaɪtəm] 餐点品种	**[座位]**	**outdoor seat** 室外座位
	price [praɪs] 餐点价钱	**indoor seat** 室内座位	
for here 内用	**smoking area** 吸烟区	**non-smoking area** 非吸烟区	**stateroom** [ˈsteɪtruːm] 包厢
to go 外带			

出发前 | 机场相关 | 国外住宿 | 观光景点 | 异国美食 | 购物乐趣 | 紧急状况 | 旅游情报

♪ 127

琳琅满目的蛋糕柜

美国是嗜好甜食者的天堂！

蛋糕有很多种，口味通常是甜的，如果从蛋糕的用途来看，可分成：生日蛋糕、结婚蛋糕等。如果从食材来看的话，蛋糕的基本材料有：面粉、糖、蛋、牛奶，再搭配其他的食材（例如：果汁、水果、翻糖、奶油等），就会成为不一样的蛋糕。

以下是几种比较具代表性的蛋糕种类：

杯子蛋糕（cup cake）

杯子蛋糕是蛋糕店的新宠，小小一份很适合一个人吃，通常杯子蛋糕上会挤上奶油，再撒上糖粉，或运用翻糖、新鲜水果做装饰。

戚风蛋糕（chiffon cake）

口感松软是戚风蛋糕的最大特色，直接吃的话，可以吃到蛋糕的原味，也有店家以戚风蛋糕为基底，在外层抹上鲜奶油，并进行蛋糕装饰。

芝士蛋糕（cheese cake）

芝士蛋糕是最常见的蛋糕之一，因为使用的芝士和烤制的方法不同，会形成不同的口感，最常见的口味有：原味、巧克力，表层较常见的装饰为草莓或蓝莓。

天使蛋糕（angel food cake）
恶魔蛋糕（devil's food cake）

两个是极大的对比，天使蛋糕的颜色雪白，口感清爽，而恶魔蛋糕则含有丰富的巧克力。

提拉米苏（tiramisù）

提拉米苏源于意大利，主要使用芝士、鸡蛋、鲜奶油、浓缩咖啡、可可粉、手指饼干制成，吃起来的口感有点像慕斯。

常见的蛋糕制作方法

◆ 打发：将蛋白、奶油、糖打发后，逐步加入其他材料。

◆ 混融：将干料混合以后，再加入融化的奶油和液体材料。

◆ 海绵：将鸡蛋和糖打发后，再加入面粉。

饼干、糖果、派!

最常见的点心,也最让人口齿留香!

饼干(cookie)

饼干的口味很多,根据拌面糊的方式及烤的方法,会有不同软硬度的口感,一般常见拌入面糊的配料有:巧克力碎片、坚果、核桃、燕麦片等。

糖果(candy)

糖果可依据口感,分为硬糖和软糖,最有名的软糖为"小熊软糖(gummy bear)"。

棒棒糖(lollipop)

棒棒糖是小孩子最喜欢的糖果之一,可以握着棒棒糖的棍子,边走边吃而不会弄脏手,而棒棒糖的颜色非常鲜艳。

幸运饼干(fortune cookie)流行于美国与加拿大,是当地中国餐厅的餐后甜点,但是在华人聚居的地区没有这道点心,更没有食用这种食物的习惯。

幸运饼干主要是用面粉、糖、香草、奶油制成,里面包有类似箴言或是预言的字条。

尚未食用的幸运饼干

把饼干剥开后,会在里面找到写有箴言或预言的纸条。

出发前 | 机场相关 | 国外住宿 | 观光景点 | 异国美食 | 购物乐趣 | 紧急状况 | 旅游情报

非吃不可的甜点

到了美国,一定要找机会吃这些甜点!

冰激凌

冰激凌(ice cream)是最常见的甜品,除了直接吃之外,它可以搭配饼干做成"甜筒"或是"冰激淋三明治"。其他常见的甜品还有口感较清爽的"雪酪(sorbet)",或是淋上各种果酱、糖浆的"圣代(sundae)"。

如果是在餐厅里面吃冰激凌的话,一般会盛在鸡尾酒杯里,并搭配鲜奶油、饼干或是水果。而源自南加州的31冰激凌(Baskin-Robbins 31 Ice Cream)以随时都能提供三十一种冰激凌闻名,目前为全世界最大的冰激凌连锁店。

甜甜圈

在很多好莱坞电影中,都可以看到里面的角色在吃甜甜圈,由此可知甜甜圈在美国的生活中是多么普遍。最常见的甜甜圈(doughnut)长得像是中空的环状,经过油炸后,撒上糖粉或肉桂粉,或是裹上糖衣。

另外也有在面团中间包入奶油或卡仕达酱等甜馅料的甜甜圈,而电影《落魄大厨》的主角带着儿子去新奥尔良买的甜甜圈,形状是方形,口感较为松软。

松饼

松饼其实是指两种不一样的食物:

❶ pancake:薄扁状,是将面糊倒进烤盘或是平底锅中,单面煎烤过后,再翻面煎烤。在食用时,可抹上奶油,或是淋上蜂蜜、果酱、巧克力酱,也可以搭配肉排食用。

❷ waffle:较pancake厚,是将面糊倒进烤模中,烤盘的上下两面有一凹一凸的花纹,因此烤出来的松饼会有格子。食用方式同pancake,可以淋上甜酱料,或是搭配咸食。

Chapter 6 购物乐趣

出国,一定要买东西!不管是品牌专卖店、百货公司,还是什么都卖的超级市场,只要带够钱、准备好信用卡,看到喜欢的就买吧!

**I buy everything I want.
I'm so lucky!**

去百货公司大采购！

有些东西在美国买，就是比较划算。

百货公司服务台

请问女装部在几楼？	Excuse me, which floor is the women's department?
在二楼。	It's on the second floor.

请问这里有纪梵希的专柜吗？	Is there the Givenchy's counter here?

在一楼入口旁。	不好意思，这里没有设柜。
It's near the entrance of the first floor.	I'm afraid we don't have this brand counter.

我想要找芭比布朗的专柜。	I'm looking for the Bobbi Brown's counter.
这个专柜在哪里？	**Could you tell me where this counter is, please?**
请问有楼层地图及店家信息吗？	**Are there the floor map and information for shops?**
我想要租借婴儿推车。	I want to rent a stroller.
请问这里有投币式的置物柜吗？	**Is there a locker here?**

♪ 132

请问电梯在哪里？	Could you show me where the elevator is?

百货公司专柜 / 品牌专卖店

不好意思，我需要帮忙。	**Excuse me, I need a favor.**
我想要找这个产品。	**I'm looking for this product.**
请问这件衬衫还有别的颜色吗？	Is this shirt in any other colors?
这件T恤有其他花样吗？	Does this T-shirt have other patterns?
我想要看那个红色背包。	I'd like to see that red backpack.
我可以看模特儿身上的那件外套吗？	May I take a look at that coat on the model?
这双鞋子是24号的吗？	Is this pair of shoes in size 24?
这件外套是什么材质？	What's the material of this coat?
这个背包防水吗？	Is this backpack water-proof?

走吧！一起用英语去旅行！

秋季新品上市了吗？	Is the autumn new arrivals on?
可以请你帮我包装成礼物吗？	Could you help me wrap as a present?
现在做什么促销活动吗？	Is there any promotion now?

试穿

我想要试穿那件连衣裙。	I'd like to try on that dress.
请问可以试穿吗？	Excuse me, may I try it on?
请问试衣间（镜子）在哪里？	Excuse me, where is the fitting room (mirror)?
我穿24号腰，这条裙子我能穿吗？	My waist is No. 24. Can I wear this skirt?
这双鞋子我穿起来不好看。	I'm not good on this pair of shoes.
这条裤子太紧。	This pair of pants is too tight.
这件衬衫有点大。	This shirt is a little bit big.

♪ 134

请给我大（小）一点的尺寸。	Please take me a bit big (small) size.
我想试穿别的颜色看看。	I'd like to try on other colors.
请问这件衬衫有别的花色吗？	Excuse me, are there any other patterns for this blouse?
我想试穿模特儿身上的上衣。	I'd like to try on the tops of the model.
请问这件连衣裙打折吗？	Excuse me, does this dress have any discounts?
不好意思，新品不打折。	Sorry that new arrivals don't have any discounts.
请问你们现在有优惠活动吗？	Do you have any promotion activities now?
这个有买二送一的活动吗？	Does it meet the activity for buying two get one free?

结账

请问是在这里结账吗？	Excuse me, can I pay here?
不好意思，我想要结账。	Excuse me, I'd like to check out.

走吧！一起用英语去旅行！

请问这全部多少钱？	How much is the total?
含不含税？	Is the tax inclusive or non-inclusive?

退税

请问消费多少可以办理退税？	**Excuse me, how much should I expend to get a tax refund?**
办理退税需要提供什么资料？	**What materials should I provide to get a tax refund?**
这是我的购物发票和护照。	Here are my shopping invoice and passport.
我要去哪里退税呢？	Where can I get a tax refund?
入口处电梯旁的柜台。	There's a tax refund counter near the escalator at the entrance.
不好意思，餐点消费无法退税。	I'm sorry that dining expense can't get a tax refund.
这笔消费可以退税吗？	**Can I get a tax refund for this expenditure?**

产品内容

请问这件裤子有新的吗？	**Do you have a new one of this pair of pants?**
请问这条项链是白金还是银制的呢？	Is this necklace made of platinum or silver?
这件连衣裙是纯棉的吗？	Is this dress pure cotton?
这是广告模特儿穿的那件牛仔裤吗？	Is this pair of jeans the same as the one which the admodel wears?
手链上的饰品是原本就附的还是要另外购买？	Does the bracelet include these accessories or need to buy additionally?

退换货

不好意思，我想要退货。	**Excuse me, I'd like to return goods.**
这个包有瑕疵，我想要换货。	There's a flaw of this purse. I'd like to exchange merchandise.
这件内衣的尺寸不合适，我想要退货。	The size of this underwear doesn't fit me. I want to return it.
不好意思，贴身衣物无法退货。	Sorry that lingerie can't be returned.

句型

_____ 在哪里?
Where is (the) _____?

[地点]

department store 百货公司	**outlet** ['aʊtlet] 折扣中心	**checking counter** 结账柜台	**elevator** ['elɪveɪtə] 电梯
	**boutique** [bu:'ti:k] 精品店		**escalator** ['eskəleɪtə] 电扶梯
locker ['lɒkə] 寄物柜	**nursery room** 哺乳室	**information counter** 服务台	**lost-and-found counter** 失物招领中心

[产品部门]

	women's department 女装部	**men's department** 男装部	**children's department** 童装部

shoe's department 鞋部	**cosmetics department** 化妆品部	**sports' department** 运动用品部	**electronic appliances** 家电
			**food court** 美食街

你们有_____吗?
Do you have a / an _____?

[衣服类]

T-shirt
['tiːʃɜːt]
T恤

sweater
['swetə]
毛衣

knit sweater
针织衫

shirt
[ʃɜːt]
衬衫

jeans
[dʒiːnz]
牛仔裤

pants
[pænts]
长裤

shorts
[ʃɔːts]
短裤

underwear
['ʌndəweə]
内衣裤

pajamas
[pə'dʒɑːməz]
睡衣

[鞋包类]

sports shoes
运动鞋

flatforms
['flætfɔːmz]
平底鞋

high heels
高跟鞋

leather shoes
皮鞋

shoulder bag
肩背包

backpack
['bækpæk]
背包

handbag
['hændbæg]
手提包

出发前 | 机场相关 | 国外住宿 | 观光景点 | 异国美食 | 购物乐趣 | 国外交通 | 紧急状况

♪139

单词

[衣物花色]

	plained ['pleɪnd] 素色	**checked** [tʃekt] 格纹	**dotted** ['dɒtɪd] 圆点
pattern ['pætn] 图案			

stripe [straɪp] 条纹

printing ['prɪntɪŋ] 印花

[袖子长度]

three quarter sleeves 七分袖

sleeves [sli:vz] 袖子

elbow-length sleeves 五分袖

long-length sleeves 长袖

short-length sleeves 短袖

sleeveless ['sli:vləs] 无袖

[尺寸]

size [saɪz] 尺寸

big [bɪg] 大的	**long** [lɒŋ] 长的	**loose** [lu:s] 宽松的	**thick** [θɪk] 厚的
small [smɔ:l] 小的	**short** [ʃɔ:t] 短的	**tight** [taɪt] 紧身的	**thin** [θɪn] 薄的

[材质]	**cotton** ['kɒtn] 棉	**linen** ['lɪnɪn] 麻	**artificial leather** 人工皮革
tactile ['tæktaɪl] 触感	**silk** [sɪlk] 丝	**chiffon** ['ʃɪfɒn] 雪纺	**genuine leather** 真皮
[衣物类型]	**coat** [kəʊt] 外套	**dress** [dres] 洋装	**purse** [pɜːs] 皮包
fashionable item 流行种类			
sunglasses ['sʌnɡlɑːsɪz] 太阳眼镜	**earrings** ['ɪərɪŋz] 耳环	**necklace** ['nekləs] 项链	**bracelet** ['breɪslət] 手镯

tie [taɪ] 领带	**hat** [hæt] 帽子	**socks** [sɒks] 袜子	**gloves** [glʌvz] 手套

出发前 | 机场相关 | 国外住宿 | 观光景点 | 异国美食 | **购物乐趣** | 国外交通 | 紧急状况

各种颜色的说法

知道颜色怎么说，才能买到想要的东西！

红色 **red** [red]

橘色 **orange** ['ɒrɪndʒ]

黄色 **yellow** ['jeləʊ]

粉红色 **pink** [pɪŋk]

紫色 **purple** ['pɜːpl]

绿色 **green** [griːn]

蓝色 **blue** [bluː]

深的 **dark** [dɑːk]

浅的 **light** [laɪt]

其他常见的颜色		**black** [blæk] 黑色	**white** [waɪt] 白色
gray [greɪ] 灰色	**brown** [braʊn] 咖啡色	**khaki** ['kɑːki] 卡其色	**camel** ['kæml] 驼色
gold [gəʊld] 金色	**silver** ['sɪlvə] 银色	**ivory** ['aɪvəri] 象牙白色	**amber** ['æmbə] 琥珀色
salmon ['sæmən] 鲑鱼红色	**lilac** ['laɪlək] 浅紫色	**navy** ['neɪvi] 藏青色	**indigo** ['ɪndɪgəʊ] 靛蓝色

四季的衣服搭配方法

一年四季该怎么穿，通通跟你说。

春天

春暖花开的日子很适合穿上单衣享受太阳的温暖，但因为气温还不够高，在阴暗处会比较凉，可以随身携带丝巾或是薄外套。男生可穿休闲裤搭配素色T恤，怕冷的话可搭配格子衬衫，就很有型了。

夏天

夏天就是穿轻薄短款衣服的季节，细肩带或是削肩背心再搭配短裙，展露性感风情。女生去海边玩的时候，别忘了穿上比基尼，男生可穿上海滩裤，展露傲人的六块腹肌。

秋天

天气变化跟春天相似，但气温较低一些，建议随身携带针织外套。不论男生或女生，都可以牛仔裤搭配短靴，再加上风衣外套，既保暖又时尚。

冬天

美国的冬天通常较为寒冷，甚至会降雪，因此羽绒衣、毛帽、围巾、雪靴、手套、耳罩是不可或缺的配备。

各种衣物的尺寸表

根据品牌不同,标示的尺码也不同,要怎么选购呢?

女性

	国际标示	XXS	XS	S	M	L	XL	XXL	
上衣	美国		32	34	36	38	40	42	44
	胸围(英寸)	32	33-34	35	36	37	38	40	41
	腰围(英寸)	24	25-26	27	28	29	30	32	33
	臀围(英寸)	35	36-37	38	39	40	41	43	44
胸罩	中国罩杯	AA	A	B	C	D	E	F	G
	美国罩杯		AA	A	B	C	D	DD	DDD / E
鞋子	中国	34	35	36	37	38	39	40	41
	美国	4 1/2	5	5 1/2	6	6 1/2	7	7 1/2	8
	英国	3 1/2	4	4 1/2	5	5 1/2	6	6 1/2	7

饰品

帽子	头围(英寸)	21 1/8-21 1/2			21 7/8-22 1/4			22 5/8-23			23 1/2-23 7/8		
戒指	国际	4	5	6	7	8	9	10	11	12	13	14	15	16
	美国	2	2.5	3	4	4.5	5	6	6.5	7	7.5	8	9	9.5
	内围总长(英寸)	4.1	4.25	4.39	4.55	4.71	4.87	5.02	5.18	5.34	5.5	5.65	5.81	5.97
	内围直径(英寸)	1.3	1.35	1.4	1.45	1.5	1.55	1.6	1.65	1.7	1.75	1.8	1.85	1.9

男性

国际标示	XS	XS	S	S	M	M	L	L	XL
美国	14	14 1/2	15	15 1/2	15 1/2	16	16 1/2	17	17 1/2
颈围（英寸）			14 1/2-15 1/4		15 1/2-16		16 1/4-16 3/4		17-17 1/4
胸围（英寸）			37-38		39-41		42-44		45-47
体围（英寸）									
肩袖长（英寸）			33		34		35		36

尺码	XS		S		M			L			XL		
体围（英寸）	28	29	30	31	32	33	34	35	36	37	38	39	40
腰带（英寸）	30		32		34		36		38		40		42

中国	38	39	40	41	42	43	44	45	
美国	6 1/2	7	7 1/2	8	8 1/2	9	9 1/2	10	10 1/2
英国	5 1/2	6	6 1/2	7	7 1/2	8	8 1/2	9	9 1/2

童装

月龄	新生儿	3个月	6个月	9个月	12个月	18个月	24个月
中国	50	60	70		75	80	90
美国	NB	3M	6M	9M	12M	18M	24M
身高（厘米）	50	60	70		75	80	90
体重（公斤）	3	6	9		10	11	13

年龄	2岁	3岁	4岁	5岁	6岁	7岁
中国	90	100	110	110	120	130
美国	2	3	4	5	6	7
身高（厘米）	85-95	95-105	105-115	115-124	115-125	115-125

药妆店是女孩们的最爱!

美国的药妆店也很好逛哦。

药妆店美妆区

我要找增长睫毛的睫毛膏。	I'm looking for the mascara for extension.
这只防水眼线笔看起来很厉害。	This water-proof eye liner looks very fantastic.
请问这款粉饼还有货吗？	Is this kind of pressed powder in stock?
有偏大地色的眼影可以推荐吗？	Can you recommend the earth tone eye shadows?
请问这是试用品吗？	**Is this for trial product?**
请问这款粉饼是4号色比3号色浅吗？	Is the color of No. 4 pressed powder lighter than No. 3?
请问这款卸妆油还会补货吗？	Will this kind of make-up remover be replenished?
架上好像没有这款眼唇卸妆液。	It seems that this kind of lip and eye remover lotion is not on the rack.
这里有脸部去角质的产品吗？	Is there any facial exfoliating scrub here?

我找不到安耐晒的防晒乳。	I can't find the sunscreen of ANESSA.
魅可的滋润护唇膏好像缺货。	It seems to be out of stock of MAC moisturizing lipstick.
整间店的彩妆都打九折吗？	Do all the cosmetics have a 10% discount in the shop?
不好意思，我看不懂这个折扣标示。	Excuse me, I don't understand the discount label.
香奈儿的指甲油并没有优惠。	There's no discount for the nail polish of CHANEL.
这里好像没有我要找的彩妆品牌。	Is seems to be no cosmetic brads that I look for here.

药妆店保养区

这里卖迪奥的保养品吗？	Are the skin care products of Dior sold here?
很多博主推荐这款保湿化妆水。	Many bloggers recommend this kind of moisturizing toner.
这款乳液适用于敏感肌肤吗？	Is this lotion suitable for sensitive skin?

走吧！一起用英语去旅行！

这是日用的还是夜用的？	Is this for day or for night?
我想要找眼霜。	I'm looking for the eye cream.
请问面膜都放在这一区吗？	Excuse me, are masks put in this section?
这是针对嘴唇的保养品吗？	Is this the skin care product for lips?
哪个是人气商品？	Which one is the best-selling item?
这款护手霜可以试用吗？	May I try this hand cream?
试用品在这里。	Samples are here.
这些面膜适合买回去送朋友。	These masks are suitable to buy for friends.
在美国，可以用不错的价钱买到一套的保养品。	You can buy a set of skin care products at such a bargain price in America.
买乳液的补充包真的很划算。	Buying the supplement packs of the lotion will really be a bargain.
这里的价钱高得多。	The price here is much higher.

我决定货比三家。	I decide to shop around.

药妆店咨询区

这沐浴乳适合干性肌肤吗？	Is this body shampoo suitable for dry skin?
我推荐你这三盒装的优惠组合牙膏。	I recommend you this three-pack preferential combination for toothpaste.
这就是更年期女性吃的营养品。	This is the nutriment for the climacteric women.
没有医生处方笺可以在这买一盒隐形眼镜吗？	Can I buy a box of contact lenses without prescription here?
请问有药剂师可以询问有关这种新药品的信息吗？	Excuse me, is there a pharmacist to ask for the information of this new drug?

药妆店药品区

请问这里卖避孕药吗？	Do you sell contraceptive drugs here?
请问感冒药放在哪一区？	Excuse me, which section is for cold medicine?

走吧！一起用英语去旅行！

不好意思，架上没有胃药了。	Sorry, there's no stomach medicine on the rack.
不好意思，店里的库存已卖完了。	I'm afraid that the stocks in the shop are sold out.
请问卖镇静剂吗？	Excuse me, do you sell sedatives?
有的，但需要有处方笺。	Yes, but I need your prescription.
请问推荐哪款疼痛药膏吗？	Which kind of sore ointment do you recommend?
我想要找眼药水。	I'm looking for the eye drops.
这两款眼药水，哪款比较凉？	Which one is much cooler between these two types of eye drops?
这款止痛药有小盒装的吗？	Is there this painkiller packed in a small box?
有 60 片、30 片、20 片装。	There are this painkller packed in sixty tablets, thirty ones and twenty ones.
麻烦请给我 30 片装的。	Please give me the pack in thirty tablets.
我想要找这款祛痘药膏。	I'd like to look for this kind of acne ointment.

药妆店杂物区

这款瘦脸按摩棒感觉很有用。	This facial massage bar seems good to use.
可以试闻这款芳香剂吗？	May I try this aromatic?
我想买包沐浴皂回饭店试试。	I want to buy a pack of bathing soap to try in the hotel.

药妆店柜台

结账是从这里排队吗？	Is the line for checking out?
如果要退税，请排3号柜台。	If you want to refund the money, please queue up at No. 3 counter.
是拿空盒去柜台结账吗？	Should I check out with the empty box at the counter?
我要两盒180片装的维生素B。	I'd like two boxes of vitamin B with one hundred and eighty tablets.
一个人最多只能买三组生理食盐水。	Everyone just can buy at most three sets of normal saline.
我可以用信用卡结账吗？	May I pay by / with credit card?
不用装塑料袋，我有购物袋。	Do not pack in a plastic bag. I have a shopping bag myself.

♪ 151

每个人只能买两罐维生素 C 吗？	Can everybody just buy two cans of vitamin C?
不好意思，每人的购买数量有限制。	I'm afraid that everyone has the limitation for the purchase quantities.
好的，我知道了。	Okay, I got it.
请多给我一个袋子。	**Please give me one more bag.**

药店服务

我的手在流血，可以帮我包扎吗？	My hand is bleeding. Can you help me to bandage it?
我被烫伤了，请帮我擦药。	I got burnt. Please do me a favor to apply on medication.
我被铁丝网割伤了，怎么办？	I was cut by the wire gauze. What should I do?

美甲店

| 我想要做光疗指甲。 | **I'd like to have gel nails done.** |
| 我想要做手和脚的基础保养。 | **I'd like to do some basic care of my hands and feet.** |

请帮我涂有亮粉的红色指甲油。	Please apply red nail polish with bright powder.
请问今天想要做哪种款式的指甲彩绘呢？	What type of nail art and painting do you like to do today?
我想做你们最新推出的童话款。	I'd like the latest type of fairy tales.

美体美容店

我想要体验蜜蜡除毛。	**I'd like to try waxing hair removal.**
请问你们有 SPA 服务吗？	Excuse me, do you have SPA service?
你可以为我介绍你们的服务吗？	Can you introduce your services for me?
你们现在有优惠活动吗？	Do you have any promotion activities now?
除毛搭配 SPA 的话，有八折优惠。	There's a twenty percent off discount if hair removal comes with SPA.

句型: 你们有_____吗？
Do you have a / an _____?

[沐浴用品]

towel ['taʊəl] 毛巾

body wash 沐浴乳

soap [soʊp] 香皂

shower sponge 沐浴球

hair shampoo 洗发乳

hair conditioner 润发乳

[卸妆用品]

facial cleanser 洗面乳

makeup remover oil 卸妆油

lip & eye remover 眼唇卸妆液

scrub [skrʌb] 去角质霜

[脸部保养]

toner ['toʊnɚ] 化妆水

lotion ['loʊʃn] 乳液

serum ['sɪrəm] 美容液

eye cream 眼霜

day cream 日霜

night cream 晚霜

lip balm 护唇膏

moisturizing lotion 滋润乳液

♪154

[身体保养]	**body lotion** 身体乳	**massage cream** 按摩霜	**body scrub** 身体磨砂膏	出发前
		wrinkle remover cream 除皱霜	**body moisturizer** 身体护肤霜	机场相关
_____在哪里？ Where is / are a (an / the) _____ ?		**best-selling section** 畅销产品区	**skin care section** 保养品区	国外住宿
cosmetics section 化妆品区 	**drug section** 药品区	**food section** 食品区 	**checking counter** 结账柜台	观光景点
			clerk [klɑːk] 店员	异国美食
我想要请问有关 _____的事情。 I'd like to ask about (the) _____.		**product information** 产品信息	**product location** 产品位置	购物乐趣
			set [sɛt] 组合	国外交通
price [praɪs] 价格	**discount** [ˈdɪskaʊnt] 折扣	**special offer** 优惠方案	**drawback** [ˈdrɔːbæk] 退税	紧急状况

♪ 155

[保养品类]

basic skin care
基础皮肤保养

toning lotion
化妆水

essence
['esns]
精华液

moisturizing lotion
保湿乳液

whitening cream
美白霜

eye cream
眼霜

hand cream
护手霜

lip balm
润唇膏

mask
[mɑːsk]
面膜

day cream
日霜

eye mask
眼膜

[保养品功效]

nutritious
[nju'trɪʃəs]
滋润的

whiten
['waɪtn]
美白

lip mask
唇膜

function
['fʌŋkʃn]
功能

moisturize
['mɔɪstʃəraɪz]
滋润

repair
[rɪ'peə]
修护

dermisa whitening
淡斑

anti-aging
['ænti 'eɪdʒɪŋ]
抗老

tighten
['taɪtn]
紧实

anti-acne
['ænti 'ækni]
抗痘

exfoliate scrub
去角质

eliminate wrinkles
除皱

skin conditioning
皮肤调理

♪ 156

[保养品成分]

collagen ['kɒlədʒən] 胶原蛋白	**Alpha Hydroxy Acids** 果酸	[肌肤特性]
natural ingredient 天然成分	**vitamin** ['vɪtəmɪn] 维生素	**hyaluronic acid** 玻尿酸	**skin** [skɪn] 肌肤
dry skin 干燥肌肤	**oily skin** 油性肌肤	**combination skin** 混合性肌肤	**sensitive skin** 敏感肌肤

[化妆品]

	foundation [faʊn'deɪʃn] 粉底	**pressed powder** 粉饼	**BB cream** BB霜
cosmetic [kɒz'metɪk] 化妆品			**concealer** [kən'siːlə] 遮瑕膏
foundation liquid 粉底液	**eye shadow** 眼影	**mascara** [mæ'skɑːrə] 睫毛膏	**eye liner** 眼线笔
make-up base 隔离霜			
liquid eye liner 眼线液	**gel eye liner** 眼线胶	**brow pencil** 眉笔	**brow powder** 眉粉

出发前 | 机场相关 | 国外住宿 | 观光景点 | 异国美食 | **购物乐趣** | 国外交通 | 紧急状况

单词

lipstick ['lɪpstɪk] 口红	**blush** [blʌʃ] 腮红	**face powder** 蜜粉	**lip liner** 唇笔
			lip gloss 唇蜜
nail polish 指甲油	**nail sticker** 指甲贴纸	[化妆品功能]	**waterproof** ['wɔːtəpruːf] 防水
	tattoo sticker 文身贴纸	**anti-oil** 防油	**smudge-shield** 防晕染
[药品]	**cold medicine** 感冒药	**painkiller** ['peɪnkɪlə] 止痛药	**gastrointestinal drug** 肠胃药
over-the-counter medicine 非处方药	**antitussive** 止咳药	**external application** 外用药	**eye drops** 眼药水
sore ointment 疼痛药膏	**eczema ointment** 湿疹药膏	**iodine** ['aɪədiːn] 碘酒	**mosquito repellent** 防蚊液
pain relieving patch 酸痛贴布	**burn medicine** 烫伤药	**pimple ointment** 粉刺药膏	**anti-mosquito patch** 防蚊贴片

insect bite 蚊虫咬伤	[药品状态]	**powder** ['paʊdə] 粉状	**tablet** ['tæblət] 片状
normal saline 生理食盐水	**ointment** ['ɔɪntmənt] 膏状		
capsule ['kæpsjuːl] 胶囊状	**box packaging** 盒装	**can packaging** 罐装	**bulk packaging** 散包装
[身体清洁]	**toothpaste** ['tuːθpeɪst] 牙膏	**toothbrush** ['tuːθbrʌʃ] 牙刷	**floss** [flɒs] 牙线
toiletry ['tɔɪlɪtrɪ] 盥洗用具			**dental flosser** 牙线棒
face wash sponge 洗脸用海绵	**washcloth** ['wɒʃklɒθ] 毛巾	**bathing powder** 沐浴粉	**acne bar** 粉刺棒
		shower powder 淋浴粉	**blemish extractor** 挤痘痘棒

单词

[头发相关]

hair conditioner 润发乳	**hair mask** 发膜	**hair straightener** 直发夹
hair shampoo 洗发乳	**hair pomade** 护发油	**hair dye** 染发剂	**hair roller** 卷发夹

hair blower 吹风机

comb [kəʊm] 梳子

flat comb 扁梳

round comb 圆梳

hair spray 定型液

hair gel 发胶

[居家小物]

toilet paper 卫生纸

hair wax 发蜡

hygiene item 清洁用品

pesticide ['pestɪsaɪd] 杀虫剂

fabric softener 衣物柔顺剂

laundry bag 洗衣袋

hanger ['hæŋə] 衣架

deodorant [di'əʊdərənt] 除臭剂

air freshener 芳香剂

[美容用品区]

skin care product 美容用品	**make-up cotton** 化妆棉	**eyebrow trimmer** 修眉刀	**shaving blade** 除毛刀 **razor** ['reɪzə] 剃须刀
powder brush 蜜粉刷	**eyebrow brush** 眉刷	**eye shadow brush** 眼影刷 	**blush brush** 腮红刷 
powder puff 粉扑 	**sponge** [spʌndʒ] 海绵	**nail clippers** 指甲钳	**manicure trimmer** 磨甲片 **polish stick** 抛光棒
eyelash curler 睫毛夹	**make-up mirror** 化妆镜 	**cotton swab** 棉花棒	**sanitary pad** 卫生棉 **tampon** ['tæmpɒn] 卫生棉条

出发前 | 机场相关 | 国外住宿 | 观光景点 | 异国美食 | 购物乐趣 | 国外交通 | 紧急状况

百货公司楼层介绍

每家百货公司的楼层配置都略有不同。

餐厅

百货公司的顶楼或是地下室会有餐厅,一般来说,地下室的餐厅类似美食街。

休闲

在这里可以看到各种休闲运动品牌,例如:Nike、Adidas、The North Face、Levi's 等。

女装

有些百货公司的女装部会依据年龄分成很多层,女性内衣也会放在这层,婴幼儿用品有时也会并入此层。

停车场

停车场或是出租车招呼站通常都位于地下室。

6 楼
5 楼
4 楼
3 楼
2 楼
1 楼
地下室

家居

寝具、家饰小物、室内芳香剂、餐具、厨具等,都可以在这里找到,好用的 Le Creuset、Staub 也是在这一个部门。

男装

男装就没有像女装分得这么细,包含西装、领带等男性用品都能在这里找到。

化妆品、鞋子

各种化妆品、保养品都在一楼,鞋子专柜也通常会在这一层。

一定要逛的超市

到国外一定要去逛量贩店，享受跟当地人一起购物的乐趣！

超市可以提供各式各样的产品，方便一般家庭采购生活用品。在国外，一般家庭会于周末开车去超市，可以采买一周所需，包含各种食材。

在美国比较知名的超市有Costco（好市多）、Walmart（沃尔玛），英国有Tesco（乐购），法国有Carrefour（家乐福）、Auchan（欧尚）。

以下是超市里会卖的东西，除了基本的食品和生活用品之外，家用电器也是超市出售的品种之一。

新鲜蔬果

生鲜鱼、肉类

食品

清洁用品

生活用品

家电

购物时常用的句型

记得这些句型，在购物的时候会非常好用哦！

我想要找_____。
I want to find _____.

你们有_____吗？
Do you have _____?

[使用情况]
可拿着事先找的产品信息询问店员，然后在空格处放入产品名称或是"this (one)（这个）"。

[使用情况]
当要请店员帮忙拿两个以上的物品时，可以使用这个句型，空格处填入产品名称即可。如果超过两个以上的话，and 放在最后一项物品前。

请给我_____和_____。
Please give me _____ and _____.
Please give me _____, _____ and _____.

你推荐哪种_____呢？
Which _____ do you recommend?

你会买哪种_____呢？
Which _____ will you purchase / buy?

[使用情况]
当想要购买某种产品，但因为产品众多，不知如何选购时，可以用这个句型询问店员。

[使用情况]
询问化妆品或保健品的适用肌肤、适用年龄等。

_____我可以用吗？
Can I use _____?

_____适合我吗？
Does this _____ suit me?

_____有试用品吗？
Do you have any _____ samples I can try?

[使用情况]
当想要试用化妆品时，可以用这个句型询问店员，同样，在空格处填入产品名称即可。

Chapter 7 国外交通

最好事先查好前往目的地的交通方式,许多大城市的地铁系统都很方便,但四通八达的地铁,也代表路线更复杂。除了地铁之外,也可以选择巴士、游览船等交通方式,会看到城市的另一个面貌。

Let me check the departure time...

四通八达的地铁系统!

掌握地铁线路及乘车路线,就能到处走走逛逛。

▎买票

请问售票处在哪里?	Excuse me, could you tell me where the ticket office is?
前面绿色招牌处就是了。	The green sign board ahead is the ticket office.
请问这里可以买到纳维戈的车票吗?	Excuse me, can I buy a NAVIGO ticket here?
可以,请问要去哪里呢?	Yes, you can. How many zones are you going to buy?
我可以在哪里储值纳维戈呢?	Where can I store the value of NAVIGO?
该如何买车票会比较划算呢?	What is the better bargain to buy the ticket?
我想买周票。	I want to buy a weekly ticket.

▎自动售票机

| 自动售票机要怎么操作? | **How could I use this ticket vending machine?** |
| 不好意思,我不会用自动售票机。 | Sorry, I can't operate this ticket vending machine. |

买两张全票的话是按这里吗？	Should I press this button if I want to buy two adult tickets?
是按这个按钮选择目的地吗？	Do I press this button to select my destination?
我想去圣母院，应该在哪里转车呢？	I plan to go to Cathedral de Notre-Dame. Which station should I transfer?
地图上的中央车站看起来似乎是可以转换其他线路。	It seems that Grand Central Terminal on the map can transfer to other lines.
这个是购票的收据吗？	Is this the ticket receipt?

询问时刻

请问可以索取时刻表吗？	Excuse me, can I get the timetable?
车子会按照上面的时间发车吗？	Does the subway leave for on schedule?
最早是什么时候发车？	What time does the early train start?
前往贝克街的末班车是几点发车？	What time does the last train leave for Baker Street?

♪ 167

车子是否有点误点了？	Is the train a little bit behind schedule?
从这里坐到蒙马特山丘要多久？	How long will it take from here to Montmartre?

询问路线

请问有地铁路线图吗？	Excuse me, do you have the subway route map?
下一站是哪一站呢？	Which station is the next one?
我想去女王公园，要坐哪一条线呢？	I'd like to go to Queen's Park. Which line should I take?
如果想去草莓园，要坐哪一条线呢？	Which line should I take if I want to go to the Strawberry Fields?
想去蓬皮杜中心的话，要坐到哪一站？	If I want to go to Centre Georges Pompidou, which station will I take to?
哪一站离卢浮宫博物馆比较近？	Which station is much closer to Louvre Museum?

我需要再转车吗？	Do I need to transfer once again?
纽约的地铁系统一点也不复杂。	The metro system in New York isn't complicated at all.

询问月台

请问往迪士尼的RER月台在哪里？	Excuse me, where is the platform of RER line heading for Disneyland?
黄线的月台要往哪里走呢？	Where should I go to the platform of the yellow line?
这班车是往香榭丽舍大道的方向吗？	Is it the direction to Champs-Elysees?
这里是往埃菲尔铁塔方向的黄线月台吗？	Is this the platform of the yellow line to the Eiffel Tower?
这班车停伦敦桥站吗？	Does this train stop at London Bridge station?
请问这里是往戴高乐机场吗？	Excuse me, is this line to Aero Port Paris-Charles de Gaulle?
请问是在这里排队搭车吗？	Excuse me, is this the line for boarding on the train?

走吧！一起用英语去旅行！

询问车站环境

请问厕所靠近哪个出口？	Excuse me, which exit is the toilet close to?
不好意思，我可以进站上个厕所吗？	Sorry that can I get in to use the toilet?
请问这个车站有哺乳室吗？	Is there the nursing room in this station?
有的，在一号出口附近。	Yes, there is one near the gate of No. 1.
请问电梯靠近几号出口？	Excuse me, which exit is close to the elevator?
三号出口有直达一楼的电梯。	There's a direct elevator to the first floor at the gate of No. 3.
这个车站只有楼梯，没有电扶梯吗？	Does this station only have stairs, without escalators?
这里的电扶梯坏了。	The escalator is broken here.
我的车票不见了，该如何出站呢？	**My ticket was gone. How could I get out of the station?**

我需要补票，要去哪里补票呢？	**I need to make up for my ticket. Where should I go?**
请问我需要补多少车费呢？	How much should I make up for the ticket fare, please?
不好意思，我想要充值。	Excuse me, I'd like to top up my card.
好的，要充值多少钱呢？	No problem. How much are you going to top up your card?
充值50美元。	It's USD 50.
这个出口会连接百货公司吗？	Does this exit connect to the department store?
我想去博物馆的话，要走一号还是三号出口呢？	**If I want to go to the museum, should I take No.1 or No.3 exit?**
地铁站可以吃东西或喝饮料吗？	Can I eat or drink in the subway station?
我应该在百老汇下车，但我买错票了。	I should get off at the Broadway station, but I bought the wrong ticket.

♪ 171

句型	这是往 _____ 的车吗? Is this the train to (the) _____ ?	[景点]	**Universal Park** 环球乐园
		Disneyland 迪士尼乐园	**cable car** 缆车

Tower Bridge 伦敦塔桥	**London Eye** 伦敦眼	**Buckingham Palace** 白金汉宫	**Westminster Abbey** 威斯敏斯特大教堂

Big Ben 大本钟	**Chateau de Versailles** 凡尔赛宫	**Arc de Triomphe** 凯旋门	**Champs-Elysees** 香榭丽舍大道
			**Cathedral de Notre-Dame** 圣母院
Eiffel Tower 埃菲尔铁塔	**Moulin Rouge** 红磨坊	**Provence** 普罗旺斯	**the Mediterranean** 地中海

[地点]

airport ['eəpɔ:t] 机场

train station 火车站

harbor ['hɑ:bə] 港口

_____ 在哪里?
Where is (the) _____ ?

[车站内部]

ticket counter 售票柜台

platform sign 月台标示

entrance ['entrəns] 入口

ticket gate 检票口

billboard ['bɪlbɔ:d] 广告牌

metro map 地铁图

exit ['eksɪt] 出口

platform ['plætfɔ:m] 月台

vending machine ['vendɪŋ məʃi:n] 自动贩卖机

[车站外部]

hotel [həʊ'tel] 旅馆

taxi stand 出租车停靠站

bus station 公交车站

electronic appliances street 电器街

cathedral [kə'θi:drəl] 大教堂

department store 百货公司

shopping mall 购物商场

出发前 | 机场相关 | 国外住宿 | 观光景点 | 异国美食 | 购物乐趣 | 国外交通 | 紧急状况

♪173

[车站]	Paris Visite 巴黎观光票	sluice gate 出入闸门	route map 路线图
NAVIGO ['navigɔu] NAVIGO 卡	ticket price 票价		
discount ticket 优惠票	pay the excess train fare 补票	conductor [kən'dʌktə] 列车员	timetable ['taɪmteɪbl] 时刻表
monthly pass 月票	return the ticket 退票	railway clerk 站员	
change [tʃeɪndʒ] 零钱	bill [bɪl] 钞票	interchange route 转乘路线	outbound ['aʊtbaʊnd] 出站
		carte orange 周票	inbound ['ɪnbaʊnd] 进站
walking route 行走路线	ask for directions 问路	[车体]	locomotive 车头
queuing route 排队路线	confirm the direction 确认路线	carriage ['kærɪdʒ] 车厢	

[行车路线]

	trunk line 主干线	circular line 环线	departure station 发车站
itinerary [aɪ'tɪnərəri] 路线	**branch line** 支线	**track** [træk] 轨道	**terminal station** 终点站

[车厢内部]

	seat [siːt] 座位	**window seat** 靠窗座位	**aisle seat** 靠走道座位
aisle [aɪl] 走道		**door** [dɔː] 车门	**window** ['wɪndəʊ] 车窗
priority seat 博爱座	**strap** [stræp] 拉环	**handrail** ['hændreɪl] 扶手	**fire extinguisher** 灭火器
			emergency button 紧急按钮
passenger ['pæsɪndʒə] 乘客	**advertisement** 广告	**flyer** ['flaɪə] 广告单	**No Cellphones!** 禁用手机!
	announce [ə'naʊns] 广播	**propaganda slogan** 宣传标语	**No eating.** 禁止饮食。

出发前 | 机场相关 | 国外住宿 | 观光景点 | 异国美食 | 购物乐趣 | 国外交通 | 紧急状况

♪ 175

单词

[乘车资讯]

ticket ['tɪkɪt] 车票

train number 车次

riding time 乘车时间

platform ['plætfɔːm] 月台

train type 车种

seat number 座位号码

boarding time 上车时间

departure location 上车地点

[列车类型]

metro ['metrəʊ] 地铁

arrival time 抵达时间

arrival location 抵达地点

tram [træm] 电车

steam train 蒸汽火车

TGV 高速列车

monorail ['mɒnəʊreɪl] 小火车

train [treɪn] 火车

couchette [kuːˈʃet] 卧铺车厢

overground train 地面火车

underground train 地下火车

[车站附近景点]

local train 普通车

flier ['flaɪə] 特快车

SNCF 法国国铁

manor ['mænə] 庄园

♪ 176

castle ['kɑːsl] 城堡	**church** [tʃɜːtʃ] 教堂	**parking lot** 停车场	**shopping street** 商店街
fountain ['faʊntən] 喷水池	**plaza** ['plɑːzə] 广场	**bus stop** 公交车站	**market** ['mɑːkɪt] 市场
video rental store 影碟出租店	**apparel store** 服饰店	**restaurant** ['restrɒnt] 餐厅	**convenience store** 便利商店
			**souvenir shop** 纪念品专卖店
museum [mjuˈziːəm] 博物馆	**gallery** ['gæləri] 美术馆	**park** [pɑːk] 公园	**bookstore** ['bʊkstɔː] 书店

river ['rɪvə] 河	**beach** [biːtʃ] 海滩	**mountain** ['maʊntən] 山	**field** [fiːld] 农田
			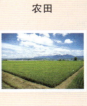

出发前 | 机场相关 | 国外住宿 | 观光景点 | 异国美食 | 购物乐趣 | **国外交通** | 紧急状况

♪ 177

纽约地铁

历史悠久、使用者多、24小时全年无休！

纽约地铁（New York City Subway）是全世界历史最悠久的地铁系统之一，拥有468座车站，目前由纽约大都会运输署管理。

纽约地铁24小时全年无休，虽说有部分车站到了晚间会关闭，但不会影响整体的营运。正是因为24小时开放，到了晚间会在车站内看到许多流浪汉。

纽约地铁的特色在于同条路线上会有三到四条轨道，中间轨道行驶的是快车（Express Service），原则上只停换乘站及终点站；左右两侧则是慢车（Local Service）使用，慢车每站皆停。

纽约地下铁路线

路线	名称	路线	名称
①	百老汇－第七大道慢车	Ⓐ	第六大道慢车
②	第七大道快车	Ⓖ	布鲁克林－皇后跨区慢车
③	第七大道快车	Ⓙ	纳苏街快车
④	莱辛顿大道快车	Ⓛ	14街－卡纳西线慢车
⑤	莱辛顿大道快车	Ⓜ	第六大道慢车
⑥ ⑥	莱辛顿大道快车/慢车	Ⓝ	百老汇慢车
⑦ ⑦	法拉盛快车/慢车	Ⓠ	百老汇快车
Ⓐ	第八大道快车	Ⓡ	百老汇慢车
Ⓑ	第六大道快车	Ⓩ	纳苏街快车
Ⓒ	第八大道慢车		42街接驳线
Ⓓ	第六大道快车	Ⓢ	法兰克林大道接驳线
Ⓔ	第八大道慢车		洛克威公园接驳线

纽约地铁将行车路径以英文字母或数字作为代号；轨道线则给予名字称呼，因此纽约地铁有"轨道线"共通组成一条"行车路径"的现象。目前纽约地铁线有24条服务路线（包含3条区间线），路线各有主色，再搭配快慢车给予代号。一般路线标示为圆圈，菱形则代表加开或快车服务的路线。

伦敦地铁

仅次于上海、北京的世界第三大地铁网络！

伦敦地铁（London Underground）于1863年通车，在伦敦市中心是地下运行，但到了郊区则转为在地面行驶。在第二次世界大战期间，许多地铁车站被充当防空洞使用。

市中心的车站在列车进站时会广播："Please mind the gap between the train and the platform."（请小心列车与月台之间的空隙。）或 "Mind the Gap."（小心空隙。）这两句话成为伦敦地铁的代表。

伦敦地铁的标示为红色圆圈、中间蓝色横杠，横杆内写 UNDERGROUND 或是地铁站名。

伦敦地下铁路线

颜色	路线	颜色	路线
	贝克卢线 Bakerloo Line		大都会线 Metropolitan Line
	中央线 Central Line		北线 Northern Line
	环线 Circle Line		皮卡迪利线 Piccadilly Line
	区域线 District Line		维多利亚线 Victoria Line
	哈默史密斯及城市线 Hammersmith & City Line		滑铁卢及城市线 Waterloo & City Line
	朱比利线 Jubilee Line	★滑铁卢及城市线在星期日及公众假期不提供服务。	

饱览街道风光的巴士！

不想坐地铁，那就乘坐巴士欣赏城市风景吧！

公交车

请问公交车站在哪里呢？	Excuse me, where is the bus stop?
在百货公司的前面。	It's in front of the department store.
下一班公交车3分钟后进站。	The next bus will be approaching in three minutes.
请问这班车到博物馆吗？	Is this bus to the museum?
请问要在哪里下车才可以乘船游塞纳河呢？	Where should I get off the bus to take the Seine cruise please?
去火车站是搭乘这个方向的车吗？	**Is this direction for the train station?**
想去中国城，要在哪站下车？	Which stop should I get off if I want to go to the Chinatown?
这班公交车会停在星辰酒店附近吗？	Does this bus stop near the Star Hotel?
我决定搭乘双层观光巴士游伦敦。	I decide to take the double decker to go sight-seeing the whole London.

我可以用交通一日券乘车吗？	Can I take the bus with a one-day pass?
可以的。	Of course, you can.
2-3天的观光巴士费用大约是100美元。	The fare of two to three days for tour bus will be around 100 dollars.
这票价也包含了游船费用。	The fare also contains cruise.

出租车

请问出租车停靠站在哪里？	Excuse me, where is the taxi stand?
请帮我拦一辆出租车，谢谢。	**Please help me to hail the taxi, thank you.**
在洛杉矶坐出租车有点贵。	It's a little bit expensive to take the taxi in Los Angeles.
通常公车站附近会有排班出租车。	There are scheduled taxis near the bus stop.
要去哪里呢？	Where to?
奥赛美术馆，谢谢。	Musee d' Orsay, please.

走吧！一起用英语去旅行！

麻烦请载我到这个地址。	**Please drive me to this address.**
麻烦请载我到帝国大厦。	Please drive me to the Empire State Building.
建议去对面乘车，方向比较顺。	I suggest you take the taxi across the street; it's the right direction.
我有点赶时间，麻烦开快一点。	**I'm a little in a hurry; please drive faster.**
我们有三件行李想放到后备箱。	We'd like to put three pieces of luggage in the trunk.
开后备箱要额外收费吗？	Do you charge extra fee if opening the trunk?
停在这里就可以了。	**Please stop here.**
麻烦请停在前面转角处。	Please stop at the corner in front.
请问总共多少钱？	**How much is the total?**
我可以索取收据吗？	May I have the receipt?

▎人力车

要不要乘坐人力车游览呢？	Do you want to take the rickshaw to go sightseeing?
一个人乘坐 20 分钟，15 美元。	**It's 15 dollars for twenty minutes each person.**
想要从哪里搭乘到哪里呢？	Where would you like to start and take to?
↓ 想从奥赛美术馆到埃菲尔铁塔。	I'd like to take from Musee d' Orsay to the Eiffel Tower.
坐两个人的话，会不会太重呢？	Is it too heavy if two persons want to take the rickshaw?

▎游览船

我想要买成人票和儿童票各一张。	I'd like to buy one normal and one children tickets.
不好意思，我想要买两张票。	Excuse me, I want to buy two tickets.
↓ 对不起，你需要事先网上预约。	Sorry, you need to book online in advance.
请问一趟航程要多久？	Excuse me, how long does it take for a ride?

走吧！一起用英语去旅行！

我有点晕船。	I'm a little seasick.
请穿上救生衣。	**Please put on the life jacket.**

马车

中央公园有游园马车可以乘坐。	There's a horse carriage tour to take in the Central Park.
搭乘一趟要25美元。	**Taking a ride costs you USD 25.**
你可以跟马车一起拍张照。	You can take a picture with the horse carriage.
一辆马车最多能坐四个人。	The horse carriage can ride up to four people.

自行车

公园旁边可以租自行车。	You can rent a bicycle next to the park.
请问租自行车需要押证件吗？	Does my ID need to be held as security when renting a bike?
不用，但要收200美元的押金。	No, but we will take 200 dollars as the deposit.

请问自行车的租借费怎么算？	How much is to rent the bike?
一个小时5美元，租整天45美元。	It's USD 5 for one hour, and USD 45 for a whole day.
你们有变速的自行车吗？	Do you have derailleur bikes?
请问你们有前面有篮子的淑女车吗？	Do you have the lady's bike with a basket?

租车

我想要租一辆休闲车。	**I'd like to rent a recreational vehicle.**
请问我可以在这里租，但在其他地方还车吗？	Can I rent the car here, but return it in other places?
请问你们自动挡的车有哪些？	What kinds of automatic cars do you have?
如果我租两天，要多少钱呢？	How much is it if I rent the car for two days?

单词

[马路相关]

pedestrian crossing
斑马线

flyover
天桥

passageway
['pæsɪdʒweɪ]
地下通道

road
[rəʊd]
马路

intersection
[ˌɪntə'sekʃn]
十字路口

pedestrian precinct
行人徒步区

bikes only
自行车专用道

lane
[leɪn]
车道

one way
单行道

traffic lights
红绿灯

street
[striːt]
街道

sidewalk
['saɪdwɔːk]
人行道

dual carriageway
双向车道

traffic signs
交通标志

alley
['æli]
巷子

block
[blɒk]
街区

[租车]

driving license
驾照

ID
[ˌaɪ'diː]
身份证件

vehicle license
汽车牌照

deposit
[dɪ'pɒzɪt]
押金

anti-theft lock
防盗锁

brake
[breɪk]
刹车

throttle
['θrɒtl]
油门

♪ 186

[方向]

	arrow ['ærəʊ] 箭头	**front** [frʌnt] 前	**rear** [rɪə] 后
direction [dəˈrekʃn] 方向			
left [left] 左	**right** [raɪt] 右	**east** [iːst] 东	**south** [saʊθ] 南
		west [west] 西	**north** [nɔːθ] 北

[交通规则]

	no crossing 禁止穿越	**no entry** 禁止进入	**watch for pedestrians** 小心行人
traffic rules 交通规则			
speed limit 限制时速	**lane reduced** 车道变窄	**construction ahead** 前方施工	**yield to pedestrians** 礼让行人
			level crossing 平交道口

♪ 187

覆盖美国本土的州际公路系统

美国公路系统的一部分,连接美国各州。

州际公路

州际公路系统(Interstate Highway System),是美国公路系统的一部分,大多属高速公路,公路全线至少四线车道。

州际公路的标志为蓝底盾形,以白字标示公路编号。依据地区不同,限速也各有不同,限速范围从每小时65英里[①](105公里)到80英里(129公里)都有。基本上,北方的限速较低,西部的限速较高;大城市附近为每小时55英里(89公里),郊区则是每小时65英里(105公里)到80英里(129公里)。

州际公路系统路线

★ 南北向道路、奇数号码,由西向东递增

5、15、17、19、25、27、29、35、37、39、43、45、49、55、57、59、65、69、71、72、75、77、79、81、83、85、87、89、91、93、95、97、99。

★ 东西向道路、偶数号码,由南向北递增

4、8、10、12、16、20、22、24、26、30、40、44、64、66、68、70、72、74、76(西段、东段)、78、80、82、84(西段、东段)、86(西段、东段)、88(西段、东段)、90、94、96、238。

① 1英里≈1.609公里。

双层巴士与出租车

除了地铁之外，巴士和出租车也是不错的交通方式。

双层巴士

有上下层载客车厢的公交车称为"双层巴士"，上下层之间有楼梯相连，楼梯通常位于车厢的中间或后面，多数公交车有两扇车门，设在车的前面和中间。

讲到双层巴士，大家最直接会想到的就是伦敦的红色双层巴士，这种巴士已经成为英国的代表。除了英国之外，许多国家也以双层巴士当作通勤工具。

另外也有种观光巴士，上层为敞篷设计，游客坐在上层可以游览城市风光。

出租车

一般在机场、车站、百货公司、旅游景点附近都有出租车搭乘处，有些地方也会有协助叫出租车的人员。如果怕在沟通地点上发生误会，可以直接把写有目的地的纸条或名片给服务人员或司机看。

为了避免发生被出租车司机绕路、敲竹杠，建议可以向司机描述目的地附近的位置或是建筑物，以示自己对于该地点很熟悉。

国内的出租车无论车上设备如何，车资计算方式都是一样的，也不需要另外支付司机小费，但如果在美国搭乘出租车，记得要提供小费，小费通常为车费的10％。有些司机可能会因为提供了车上的其他设备给乘客，而另外索费，在司机提供这类服务之前，可以先问清楚是否需要额外支付费用。

事先查询车资

搭出租车前可先查询车资哦!

taxi fare finder

目的地　出发地　计算车资

TaxiFareFinder（http://www.taxifarefinder.com/main.php?city=Orlando）是一个可以试算出租车车资的网站，使用方法非常简单：

Step 1 输入出发地与目的地
　　　　可以用打字输入地址，也可以在地图上选择地点

Step 2 按 Get Fare（计算车资）

Step 3 网页左边会出现路程的距离、车资的报价区间、车行电话

搭乘出租车时的相关会话

- Could you organize a taxi for me to the train station?
  你可以帮我安排去火车站的出租车吗？

- Could you book a taxi to take me to the airport this afternoon, please?
  你可以帮我预订今天下午去机场的出租车吗？

- Could you hail a taxi for me, please?
  可以请你帮我叫一台出租车吗？

- Could you take me to the Empire State Building, please?
  你可以载我去帝国大厦吗？

- Could you take me to "The Yard Coffee" on the Fifth Avenue, please?
  你可以载我去第五大道的"院子咖啡"吗？

- How much is the fare, please? / How much do I owe you?
  车费多少钱？

Chapter 8 紧急状况

出国难免会碰到要寄信、取钱或是失窃、生病等状况。在紧急与困难之中，如果会几句关键的会话，对于问题的解决会非常有帮助！若遇到比较重大的意外，也可以和使馆联系。

I have no money...

寄信、取钱，一次搞定！

取个钱，买个纪念品，寄回家给家人惊喜吧！

▌银行提款

你好，我想要取钱。	Hello, I'd like to withdraw some money from my account.
好的，请问要提取多少钱？	No problem. How much are you going to withdraw?
我的银行卡在欧洲可以使用吗？	May I use my ATM card in Europe?
请问跨国提款要手续费吗？	Does it have any fee for transnational withdrawal?
每家银行的跨国提款手续费不同。	The transnational withdrawal fees are different from every bank.
海外提款密码是什么？	What is the code of overseas withdrawal?
没有密码的话，就无法提款吗？	Without a secret code, can't I draw any money from my account?
是的，不好意思。	Absolutely, I'm sorry.

♪ 192

换钱

| 请问这里可以换钱吗? | Excuse me, can I exchange some money here? |

| 能帮我将一千欧元换成小面额纸钞吗? | **Could you break a thousand euro into small bills?** |

| 麻烦给我4张100元、5张50元的钞票。 | Please give me four hundreds and then five fifties. |

| 钞票还有哪些面额呢? | What do denominations of the bills come in? |

| 请问收手续费吗? | **Do you charge any commission?** |

汇钱

| 我想要汇款到这个账户。 | I'd like to make a remittance to this account. |

| 我需要填写汇款单吗? | Do I need to fill in the transfer slip? |

193

走吧！一起用英语去旅行！

汇款的手续费是多少呢？	How much is the remittance fee?
请问哪里可以拿到汇款单？	Excuse me, where can I get a remittance note?
电梯旁的柜台。	It's at the counter next to the elevator.
麻烦帮我确认资料是否正确。	Please check whether the data is correct or not.
金额可以写阿拉伯数字吗？	Can I fill in the amount of money in in Arabic numerals?

寄件

这里可以寄明信片吗？	**Can I send postcards here?**
你们有代寄明信片的服务吗？	**Do you have the service to send postcards?**
寄明信片到中国需要多少邮资？	What's the postage to send a postcard to china?
我想要买45分的邮票。	I'd like to have a forty-five-cent stamp, please.

请给我两张永久邮票。	Please give me two forever stamps.
你好，我想寄这个包裹。	**Hello, I'd like to send this parcel.**
包裹是称重计算运费吗？	Does the package estimate the postage by scaling?
空运和平邮，哪个更加划算？	Which is the better bargain, by airmail or by surface mail?
寄空运多久会送达呢？	How long will it take by airmail?
里面是易碎品，请小心轻放。	Please place it carefully; those are breakables inside.
我可以指定送达日期吗？	**Can I designate the arrival date?**
我选择以冷藏寄送。	I choose to send by cold storage.

▎信用卡挂失

不好意思，我想挂失信用卡。	**Excuse me, I'd like to report my lost credit card.**
我的信用卡不见了，我要挂失。	My credit card was lost. I'd like to report it.

走吧！一起用英语去旅行！

我可以申请补办信用卡吗？	Can I request for a new credit card?
挂失信用卡有什么手续吗？	What's the procedure of reporting a credit card?

▎信用卡刷卡

为什么我的信用卡无法使用？	**Why can't I use my credit card?**
麻烦请帮我查询我的余额。	Please do me a favor to check my balance.
不好意思，这张卡的余额不足，无法使用。	Sorry that the balance of this card is insufficient and it can't be used.
好的，请帮我刷另外一张卡。	Okay, please swipe another card.

▎支票兑现

你好，我想要兑现这张支票。	**Hello, I'd like to cash this check.**
请问这里可以兑现支票吗？	Can I cash this check here?

| 我能在银行兑现支票吗？ | Can I cash this check in the bank? |

| 这张 200 元的支票，给你两张 100 元可以吗？ | It's a two-hundred-dollar check. Can I give you two one-hundred notes? |

| 请给我一张 100，两张 50，谢谢。 | Please give me a one-hundred note and two fifty-dollar notes. |

| 请问兑现支票需要手续费吗？ | Do you charge any surcharge when I cash the check? |

彩票

| 我想要买一张刮刮乐。 | **I'd like to buy a scratch-off lottery ticket.** |

| 这期大乐透什么时候开奖呢？ | When will it draw the winning numbers of the lottery of this term? |

| 这期大乐透的奖金有多少？ | How much will the premium of the lottery of this term be? |

句型	我可以寄_____吗？ Can I send (a / an) _____?	**vegetables** ['vedʒtəblz] 蔬菜	**food** [fuːd] 食物

postcard ['pəʊstkɑːd] 明信片	**letter** ['letə] 信件	**parcel** ['pɑːsl] 包裹	**carton** ['kɑːtn] 纸箱

electric rice cooker 电饭锅	**vacuum cleaner** 吸尘器	**oven** ['ʌvn] 烤箱	**computer** [kəm'pjuːtə] 电脑

SLR camera 单反相机	**Polarorid** 拍立得相机	**liquor** ['lɪkə] 烈酒	**wine** [waɪn] 淡酒
		smoked [ˌsməʊkd] 烟熏的	**beer** [bɪə] 啤酒

hair dryer 吹风机	**iPad** ['aɪpæd] iPad 平板电脑	**microwave** ['maɪkrəweɪv] 微波炉	**stool** [stuːl] 马桶

[邮局]

[邮局]	**envelope** [ˈenvələʊp] 信封	**stamp** [stæmp] 邮票	**mailbox** [ˈmeɪlbɒks] 邮筒
printed product 印刷物			
recipient name 收件人姓名	**recipient address** 收件人地址	**[银行]**	**bankbook** [ˈbæŋkbʊk] 存折
sender name 寄件人姓名	**sender address** 寄件人地址	**teller** [ˈtelə] 银行出纳员	
VISA card VISA 卡	**MasterCard** 万事达卡	**credit card number** 信用卡号码	**issue bank** 发卡银行
expiration date 有效期限	**authorization code** 安全码	**payment deadline** 缴款期限	**account date** 出账日期
ATM 提款机	**withdrawal slip** 提款单	**statement** [ˈsteɪtmənt] 交易明细表	**passbook entry machine** 存折补登机
	transfer slip 汇款单	**available balance** 可用余额	**bill counting machine** 点钞机

出发前 | 机场相关 | 国外住宿 | 观光景点 | 异国美食 | 购物乐趣 | 国外交通 | 紧急状况

♪ 199

不怕一万，只怕万一！

出门在外，个人的物品要保护好，同时注意身体健康。

东西丢失

咦？我的背包不见了。	Well? I've lost my backpack.
我把相机忘在公交车上了。	I left my camera on the bus.
我好像把钱包忘在餐厅里了。	I seemed to have left my purse in the restaurant.
糟糕，我把购物袋忘在地铁上了。	Whoops! I left my shopping bag on the subway.
请问你看到我的手机了吗？	Excuse me, did you see my cellphone?
请问你看到一个红色背包了吗？	Excuse me, did you see a red backpack?
请问有人捡到我的尼康相机吗？	Excuse me, did somebody pick up my Nikon camera?
请留下联系方式，捡到失物会联系你。	Please leave your contact information. When we find it, we will contact you.

遭到盗窃

我的皮夹被偷走了。	My wallet was stolen.
我的包被割破，钱包被偷了。	My bag was cut and somebody stole my purse.
刚刚在地铁上，有人偷了我的相机。	Somebody just stole my camera on the metro.
我放在脚边的包不见了。	My bag, which placed by my leg, was gone.
我放在外套口袋里的手机被偷了。	My cellphone which I put in my pocket of the coat was stolen.
那个男子抢了我的包就跑了。	That man grabbed my bag and ran away.
有人拿刀指着我，抢走了我身上所有的钱。	Somebody pointed me with a knife and robbed all my money.
旅馆房间的门锁被撬开了。	Someone pried the lock of the door open in the hotel.
我放在房间保险箱里的戒指被偷了。	The ring which I put in the safe deposit in my bedroom was stolen.

♪ 201

有人趁我们不在时进入房间偷窃。	Somebody sneaked into our room while we were not in.
不好意思，我要报案。	Excuse me, I'm going to report a case.
警察先生，我被抢劫了。	I was robbed, police officer.
地铁上有很多惯偷，要小心。	There are many habitual thieves in the subway; be careful.

证件遗失

我的护照不见了，怎么办？	My passport is missing. What should I do?
我要去哪里补办护照呢？	Where should I request for a new passport?
补办护照需要提供什么资料？	What kind of data should I provide if applying for a new passport?
我什么时候可以拿到我的新护照呢？	When can I get my new passport?

发生意外

我的脚踝好像扭到了。	My ankle seemed to be sprained.
我不小心从楼梯上摔下来了。	I fell down the stairs accidently.
我被路上的自行车撞到了。	I was hit by a bike on the street.
我碰到重型摩托车的排气管,脚被烫到了。	I touched the pipe of the heavy motorcycle, and my leg was burnt.
救命啊!我被困在电梯里了。	Help! I was stuck in the elevator.
请帮我打电话叫救护车。	Please help me call an ambulance.
请帮我叫警察。	Help me call the police, please.

生病就医

我生病了。	I got sick.
我的身体有点不舒服。	I feel a little bit uncomfortable.

走吧！一起用英语去旅行！

我从昨天拉肚子到现在。	I have got diarrhea since yesterday.
我好像发烧了。	It seems that I've got a fever.
我头痛欲裂。	I have a splitting headache.
我对贝类的海鲜过敏。	I'm allergic to seashell seafood.
我的血型是B型。	My blood type is type B.
我的手被蜜蜂螫到后就肿起来了。	My hand was stung by a bee and got swollen.
我的头好晕，感觉想吐。	**My head is dizzy which makes me feel like vomiting.**
这个伤口要缝吗？	Does this wound be stitched?
不用，只要贴人工皮。	No, it just applies the Hydrocolloid Dressings.
我的手指头被热汤烫伤了。	My finger was scalded by the hot soup.
我需要打针吗？	Do I have to get an injection?
可以麻烦你开感冒药给我吗？	Can you prescribe some cold medicine for me?

这是处方笺，去药店买药就可以了。	Here is the prescription. Go to the drug store and take the medicine.
好的，谢谢你。	Okay, thank you.
我需要住院治疗吗？	Do I need to be hospitalized to be cured?
住院观察比较好。	It will be better to be in hospital for observations.
可以请你开诊断证明书吗？	Could you prescribe me a medical certificate?

打电话

哪里有公共电话呢？	**Where is the public telephone?**
要怎么打电话回中国呢？	How could I make a call to China?
我想买国际电话卡。	I'd like to buy an international phone card.
你好，我想查询博物馆的电话号码。	Hi, I want to consult the telephone number of the museum.
好的，号码是02-23457222。	All right, the number is 02-23457222.
我可以打对方付费的电话吗？	Can I make a collect call?

♪ 205

句型	请问捡到_____了吗? Excuse me, did somebody pick up (a / an) _____ ?	**billfold** [ˈbɪlfəʊld] 皮夹 	**coin purse** 零钱包
backpack [ˈbækpæk] 双肩背包 	**shoulder bag** 肩背包 	**handbag** [ˈhændbæg] 手提包 	**suitcase** [ˈsuːtkeɪs] 行李箱
camera [ˈkæmərə] 相机 	**mobile phone** 手机 	**smart phone** 智能手机 	**tablet PC** 平板电脑 
MP3 player MP3播放器 	**notebook** [ˈnəʊtbʊk] 笔记本 	**passport** [ˈpɑːspɔːt] 护照 **visa** [ˈviːzə] 签证	**credit card** 信用卡 **traveler's check** 旅行支票

[紧急状况]

police station 警察局	**police post** 派出所	**cop** [kɒp] 警察

emergency [ɪˈmɜːdʒnsɪ] 紧急状况

police [pəˈliːs] 警察

ambulance [ˈæmbjələns] 救护车	**paramedic** [ˌpærəˈmedɪk] 急救医生	**hospital** [ˈhɒspɪtl] 医院	**pharmacy** [ˈfɑːməsi] 药店

emergency room 急诊室

[生病]

	headache [ˈhedeɪk] 头痛	**stomachache** [ˈstʌməkeɪk] 胃痛	**sitotoxism** 食物中毒
symptom [ˈsɪmptəm] 病状	**toothache** [ˈtuːθeɪk] 牙痛	**diarrhea** [ˌdaɪəˈrɪə] 拉肚子	**food allergy** [fuːd ˈælədʒi] 食物过敏
cold [kəʊld] 感冒	**cough** [kɒf] 咳嗽	**asthma** [ˈæsmə] 气喘	**fracture** [ˈfræktʃə] 骨折
fever [ˈfiːvə] 发烧	**have a runny nose** 流鼻涕	**sprain** [spreɪn] 扭伤	**cut** [kʌt] 割伤

如何在美国对外联络

公共电话

由于手机的普及,路上可见的公共电话数量日渐减少,现有的多半会位于便利店、街角、餐厅或是交通转运的地方。美国的公用电话在每台话机上都写上了该话机的号码,除了拨打还可以接听。通话费用的付费方式有以下两种:

投币 当地电话投 25 美分,长途电话投 50 美分,话机不接受 1 分钱的硬币。

预付卡 在美国当地都可以购买国际电话卡,但使用前须先确认该话机是否支持国际通话。

除了自行拨号之外,还可以按下 0 或 00 请接线员代拨,通话费用可以是自费或是对方付费(collect call),付费方式通常为信用卡。而美国和加拿大的求救电话为 911、英国为 999 或是 112、澳大利亚为 000、新西兰为 111。

拨号方式

拨打美国电话
❶ 当地电话:1 + 区域号码 + 7 位电话号码
❷ 免付费(Toll-free)电话:1 + 800 + 7 位电话号码

拨打国际电话
❶ 拨打电话:011 + 国码 + 区码 + 电话号码
❷ 拨打手机:011 + 国码 + 手机号码

信件格式

寄件人姓名
寄件人地址
寄件人国名

收件人姓名
收件人地址
收件人国名

紧急救难资讯

紧急联络资讯一定要铭记在心！

	中国驻美国大使馆
地址	3505.International place, NW, Washington, D.C.2008
联系方式	(202) -495-2266 (202) -669-8024（非工作时间及假期，仅供紧急联络使用） (202) -495-2138（传真）
受理时间	周一～周五，上午 9 点到下午 5 点

中国驻美国领事馆

芝加哥（Chicago）
电话：
(312) 18030095

洛杉矶（Los Angeles）
电话：
(213) 8078088

旧金山（San Francisco）
电话：
(415) 6742900

休斯敦（Houston）
电话：
(713) 5219996

纽约（New York）
电话：
(212) 2449456

找寻人事物

Where is (the)...? ……在哪里？
I'm looking for (the / a / an)... 我在找……

人物

- 航空乘务人员
  flight attendant
- 地勤人员
  the ground staff
- 站务员
  station staff
- 店员
  clerk
- 服务人员
  receptionist
- 司机
  driver
- 警察
  policeman
- 医生
  doctor

地点

- 机场
  airport
- 酒店
  hotel
- 游泳池
  swimming pool
- 淋浴间
  showering room
- 健身房
  gymnasium (gym)
- 更衣间
  fitting room
- 结账柜台
  check-out counter
- 停车场
  parking lot
- 出租车停靠站
  taxi stand
- 公交车站牌
  bus stop sign
- 地铁站
  metro station
- 警察局
  police station

物品

- 电梯
  elevator
- 手扶梯
  escalator
- 楼梯
  stairs
- 天桥
  overpass
- 人行道
  pavement
- 插座
  outlet
- 自动提款机
  automated teller machine
- 充值机
  add value machine

观光景点

- 美术馆
  art museum
- 博物馆
  museum
- 天文馆
  planetarium
- 游乐园
  amusement park
- 水族馆
  aquarium
- 植物园
  botanical garden
- 科学馆
  science museum
- 观景台
  scenic overlook
- 国家公园
  national park
- 度假村
  resort
- 瀑布
  waterfall
- 吊桥
  suspension bridge
- 滑雪场
  skiing resort

表达需求

> **I want to...** 我想要做……
> **I want (a / an) ...** 我想要……

动作

- 登记入住
  check in
- 退房
  check out of the room
- 点一份沙拉
  order a salad
- 找东西吃
  find something to eat
- 结账
  check out
- 刷卡结账
  pay by / with credit card

- 试穿
  try on
- 换其他尺寸
  change another size
- 玩过山车
  ride on the roller coaster
- 乘坐摩天轮
  ride on the Ferris wheels
- 骑自行车
  ride a bicycle
- 划船
  row a boat

物品

- 枕头
  pillow
- 毛毯
  blanket
- 耳机
  headphones
- 吹风机
  hair dryer

- 加湿机
  humidifier
- 除湿机
  dehumidifier
- 变压器
  adaptor
- 遥控器
  remote control

- 收音机
  radio
- 黑胶唱片机
  gramophone record machine

请求协助

Please help me... 请帮我……

动作

- 拍照
  take a picture
- 点餐
  order a meal
- 预约餐厅
  book a restaurant
- 购买车票
  buy a ticket
- 修改裤长
  amend the length of pants
- 拿新的那件
  take the new one
- 打电话给 911
  call 911
- 叫救护车
  call the ambulance

禁止

Don't... 不要……
No + V-ing. 禁止……

- 抽烟
  smoke
- 饮食
  drink
- 奔跑
  run
- 大声喧哗
  make a racket
- 拍照
  take a picture
- 使用闪光灯
  use the flashlight
- 使用脚架
  use the tripod
- 录影
  record

版权专有　侵权必究

图书在版编目（CIP）数据

走吧！一起用英语去旅行！／林雨薇著.—北京：北京理工大学出版社，2019.5
　ISBN 978-7-5682-6898-1

Ⅰ.①走… Ⅱ.①林… Ⅲ.①英语－口语－自学参考资料 Ⅳ.①H319.9

中国版本图书馆CIP数据核字（2019）第059095号

北京市版权局著作权合同登记号图字：01-2017-5668
简体中文版由我识出版社有限公司授权出版发行
走吧！一起用英语去旅行！，林雨薇著，2015年，初版
ISBN：9789869203760

出版发行 /	北京理工大学出版社有限责任公司	
社　　址 /	北京市海淀区中关村南大街5号	
邮　　编 /	100081	
电　　话 /	(010)68914775(总编室)	
	(010)82562903(教材售后服务热线)	
	(010)68948351(其他图书服务热线)	
网　　址 /	http://www.bitpress.com.cn	
经　　销 /	全国各地新华书店	
印　　刷 /	河北鸿祥信彩印刷有限公司	
开　　本 /	787毫米×1092毫米　1/32	
印　　张 /	7	责任编辑 / 龙　微
字　　数 /	186千字	文案编辑 / 龙　微
版　　次 /	2019年5月第1版　2019年5月第1次印刷	责任校对 / 杜　枝
定　　价 /	32.00元	责任印制 / 李志强

图书出现印装质量问题，请拨打售后服务热线，本社负责调换